STUDYING FILMS

ALSO AVAILABLE IN THIS SERIES

STUDYING BOLLYWOOD

Garret Fay

Garret Fay has worked as a teacher in Bedfordshire, UK, for over a decade as both Head of Faculty for Creative Arts and as a Head of Media and Film Studies.

Dedication
For the three most important women in my life: Helen, Imogen and Irene.

First published in 2011 by
Auteur, The Old Surgery, 9 Pulford Road, Leighton Buzzard LU7 1AB
www.auteur.co.uk
Copyright © Auteur 2011

Series design: Nikki Hamlett
Set by Cassels Design www.casselsdesign.co.uk
Printed and bound by Direct Printing, Wellingborough, UK

British Library Cataloguing-in-Publication Data
A catalogue record for this book is available from the British Library

ISBN 978-1-906733-07-0

Contents

Introduction

Unlocking Bollywood is not insurmountable for students, but it is daunting. The cultural proximity of Italian Neo-Realism in the 1940s or the French New Wave of the 1960s makes these European film movements slightly easier to access. Bollywood doesn't have that cultural proximity to aid students in their understanding of the texts. When you combine the language barrier and the specific narrative functions of this particular world cinema style, you compound the difficulties that students have in unlocking Bollywood films. In this text I hope to provide students, professionals and academics with a clear understanding of exactly what Bollywood is as an art form and as a global media institution.

In this text I have condensed the information in order to give a clear and accessible snapshot of the necessary elements of Bollywood, both - past and present. In approaching Bollywood, I have identified the questions that my students ask me. Typically they are related to the song and dance routines in the films, why they look so poorly produced and what language they are speaking.

But once you have started to scratch the surface you quickly enter discussions on the contextual, ideological, historical and institutional complexities of Bollywood. For example, film output causes a stir; Bollywood's prolific eight hundred films a year, 10 billion dollar industry shocks most students. They are genuinely surprised by the international market and the fact that the UK's three major cinema chains all run either a Hindi night or give over a full screen access to a normal run of a Bollywood film. They are even more surprised when they realise that this is not just in the areas nationally where they perceive there to be a large sub-continental audience for the films.

How can we easily categorise this alien filmic form that throws together melodramatic stories, imperfect acting, non-sync sound (dubbing), dance routines and musical routines (where playback singers are used) and fanatical national and international non-resident audiences? To begin this categorisation we need to acknowledge the vehicle of the *masala* mix of different Indian traditions and cultural expressions that are all neatly wrapped up in the popular Hindi film. This is a filmic form which is mass produced and rubber stamped in Mumbai, the home of Indian cinema, but better known as Bollywood.

You do, however, also need to be aware of the cultural and historical formulations that have led to the popular Hindi film and its subsequent evolution since *Alam Ara* (*The Beauty of the World*, Irani, 1931) in 1931. In many ways, I hope that this book outlines the historical, cultural and evolutionary aspects of Bollywood for the reader, but that still doesn't actually answer the question that students will be asking, 'yeah, but what is Bollywood?'

James Monaco, in the first three editions of his *How to Read a Film*, simply writes off Bollywood. In the 1981 edition he says of Indian cinema:

> Like Japan, India has long had a prolific film industry. The staple of Indian cinema is the lengthy, highly stylised Musical, which still remains to be introduced to the world market. In the late fifties however, one filmmaker – Satyajit Ray – began producing films with more universal appeal. The Apu Trilogy (*Pather Panchali* 1955; *Aparajito*, 1957; *The World of Apu* 1959) was immediately appreciated in the West and Ray has become a favourite of film festivals and art houses with such films as *The Music Room* (1958), *Kanchenjunga* (1962), *Days and Nights in the*

Forest (1970) and *Distant Thunder* (1973). (Monaco, 1981, pp. 257-258)

In 1981, this might have been a reasonable assessment of Indian cinema. Its appeal would have been limited and the world's population wasn't as mobile as it is today. The cinema industry then, as now, was dominated by the Hollywood-style narrative and the Hollywood traditions that are still commercially viable. Monaco's response is also not that unusual considering how further down the aesthetic food chain Bollywood has previously believed to be in the West.

While the parallel Indian cinema has had near continual critical acclaim since the release of Sanjit Ray's *Pather Panchali* in the 1950s and provocative films like Shekhar Kapur's *Bandit Queen* in the 1990s, Bollywood has eluded the mainstream critical praise that, in the case of many films, it deserves. However, by the turn of the century many of these critically ignored films were massively popular internationally, and in 2001, Aamir Khan's post-colonial *Lagaan* was even Oscar nominated. Despite all this international activity and the increased demand for Bollywood films by non-resident Indians internationally, Monaco didn't change the short, unrepresentative paragraph on Indian cinema in the third edition of *How to Read a Film* in 2000, nor in his fourth edition published in 2009.

Every film and media department in the country will have this book on its shelf and extra copies in the school library. I, in fact, suggest it as one of the best books for students to buy. But the lack of any revision in such a popular text can only serve to perpetuate the issues that Western audiences have with Bollywood. As a result, Mike Myers' 2008 comedy *The Love Guru* (Schnabel, 2008) and Jimi Mistry's 2002 film *The Guru* (Mayer, 2002) represent a false and demeaning cultural connection of Indian film for many Western audiences. Neither of these two films are in any way Bollywood, nor do they pretend to be. But their less than respectful depiction of Indian characters and cultural issues serves to perpetuate the views of Western mainstream audiences about Indian culture and therefore Bollywood.

A recent British film does, however, act as a more favourable conduit between Western film and Bollywood. Based on Vikas Sawarup's book *Q&A* (the reference text for this book was the re-titled second edition) (Swarup, 2009) Danny Boyle's and Loveleen Tandan's *Slumdog Millionaire* (2008) is also not a Bollywood film. Nor is it Indian parallel cinema. It is an independent British film financed by Celador Films, Film4 and Pathé Films. Yet as an introduction to Bollywood it offers students a clear way into the specific cultural differences that Bollywood has. *Slumdog Millionaire* was the undeniable darling of the 2008/9 autumn and spring awards cycle. The film cleared up at the Academy Awards and the BAFTAs. As a result of its success and how well it has worked for me in the classroom, *Slumdog Millionaire* will act as an introduction to this exploration of Bollywood cinema, hopefully making the connections between the film, Indian parallel cinema and what exactly Bollywood is.

Unlocking Bollywood has traditionally been an arduous and frustrating process. I used to begin teaching it with Mani Ratnam's excellent *Dil Se* (*From the Heart*, Ratnam, 1998) but the unlikely success of *Slumdog* has made my teaching of Bollywood considerably more interactive and stimulating.

There is a hype that surrounds Danny Boyle's film that evokes classical concepts of the fairytale. The film almost wasn't distributed in theatres, yet managed to attract immense international attention and awards (the film has won one

Slumdog Millionaire

hundred and eight awards to date). The story of the film, unsurprisingly, is the key to this connection with its audiences. It is not, however, a Bollywood or an Indian parallel cinema text. So why then include a British film in a book on Bollywood? Simple – the film has many aspects of Bollywood and Indian parallel cinema narrative structures and techniques embedded in its construction, possibly due to the involvement of its co-director, Loveleen Tandan. Tandan is an accomplished parallel practitioner and was also the second unit director on Nair's *Monsoon Wedding* (2001).

The use of Hindi-speaking actors, especially the younger children, helps to create the atmosphere of a world cinema text, interspersed with English language conversations with the older characters retelling the flashbacks of the narratives. In fact I feel it is important to remember that one third of *Slumdog Millionaire* is in Hindi. This means that from an educational point of view this text could be used to introduce students' engagement with actual Bollywood texts.

The film's popularity will mean that students will have heard of it and be aware of its wide audience, therefore empowering them to feel able to watch it and read the text even though it feels foreign to them at times. But there are a few drawbacks to this approach. First, as already mentioned, it is not a Bollywood or a parallel text and a student's failure to understand this could greatly undermine their ability to fully discuss and appreciate the Bollywood genre. Another more pertinent issue is the need to enquire as to which other subject areas, especially at secondary level, are using the text. It is fully possible that departments ranging from Religious Education, General Studies and through to English may utilise it. If this is the case, the students will need to be reintroduced to the film with the parameters of the viewing made explicitly clear.

This book is not about *Slumdog Millionaire*. However, it will be appropriate to make some particular points about the film that are important to its relationship to Bollywood and Indian cinema as a whole. In production terms, at its heart, it is a British film. Celador Films and Film4 are the two major production companies behind it while Pathé Film International took up the international distribution rights.

Initially, it was to be distributed in the US by Warner Bros' independent wing, Warner Independent, which paid $5m for the US distribution rights. But in May of 2008 Warner Bros shut down its independent wing - this was a huge blow to the film as it had to be marketed in the US if it was to do well. Warner Bros suggested a straight-to-DVD launch in the US while Pathé consolidated the film's international distribution. In August of 2008, Christian Colson of Celador Films persuaded Warner Bros to sell the rights to Fox Searchlight at a knockdown $2.5m. It was this deal that made the film move in the US. Following successful festival screenings, Fox Searchlight distributed to ten independent screens initially. Fox Searchlight's faith in the film's mainstream ability led to its nationwide US release and subsequent fairytale appearance at awards ceremonies. So *Slumdog Millionaire* is a British film but one which, without doubt, benefited greatly from an American studio's distribution muscle.

So how can looking at *Slumdog* usefully serve as an introduction to Bollywood? It is actually the differences between them that is instructive. Bollywood films are made for domestic audiences, Hindi speakers in the first place and then dubbed into other national languages. The pace of the language coupled with the use of subtitles makes them hard to follow. *Slumdog Millionaire* begins in Hindi, and approximately one third of the film is in the language, but it is far more accessible. Its subtitles are of a far superior quality to those of traditional Bollywood releases. They are also in different places on the screen, making them easier to focus on. The Hindi language flashback sections of the film are also intermingled with the present, by the police interrogation and quiz show scenes. This clever use of the present actually gives the audience a break from the subtitles and as a result keeps them engaged. While we normally hear some 'Hinglish' (Chopra, 2007, p. 60) in Bollywood films, in *Slumdog Millionaire* the split between the language is distinct.

Another helpful difference between *Slumdog Millionaire* and Bollywood films lies in the sheer quality of the print. My students were amazed to discover that *Dil Se* was a late 1990's film because the quality of the print is just so poor. *Slumdog Millionaire* is a very well-constructed film and it is unsurprising that Anthony Dod Mantle won an Oscar for his cinematography. The use of a range of filters to show the differing time periods is a typically Western device that communicates very well to audiences. It would be unfair to say that all Bollywood films are characterised by poor cinematography - *Lagaan* and *K3G* (Johar, 2001) are beautifully shot for example - but the norm can look dated and of poor quality. When you link this to poor quality prints the results can look quite inferior to Western prints.

The similarities between *Slumdog Millionaire* and Bollywood are not as clear. The use of the Hindi sections are, of course, comparable; however, they are probably closer to Indian parallel cinema like *Monsoon Wedding*. The film does have connections to Bollywood; AR Rahman, the great Bollywood composer, composed the music and the famous Bollywood actor Anil Kapoor plays the evil quiz master Prem. But it is these tenuous connections between the Westernised text and the Bollywood tradition that draw attention to the differences. It means that immediately after the film ends you can confidently tell pupils that this is *not* Bollywood. The absence of any song and dance sequences is the clearest reason for this. There is the dance at the end of the film to 'Jai Ho', but this is not a Bollywood dance sequence. The hero and heroine don't share a song. A courtship is not tentatively enacted through song and dance as it would be in a *masala* mix, Bollywood film.

This separation of *Slumdog Millionaire* and Bollywood films in essence allows students to see exactly how Western films differ from Bollywood films. I normally play a compilation of Bollywood film clips at this stage to reinforce this point. *Slumdog Millionaire* therefore acts as a great introduction to Bollywood without actually being a Bollywood film.

The structure of this book is designed to provide the reader with the underpinning knowledge and understanding. The text will explore key moments in Indian history to contextualise the nation of India. This will lead into a discussion of the early years of Indian cinematic history before the arrival of the first *masala* talkie, *Alam Ara* in 1931.

Having established the historical context the text will then move into a chronological analysis of the industry from the

1940s to the present day. In order to achieve this and also analyse the key texts and auteurs of the industry, I have focused on key directors and actors in these periods and their key films. The text should aid the study of Bollywood as a national cinema style. It should also provide the historical depth needed to really understand the Bollywood cinema industry.

India: From corporation to colony to nuclear power

The East India Company

India 1783 under the influence of the East India Company

India was a prize for the European traders of the 15th century. The Dutch, Portuguese and the English all sought to establish a foothold in the country. The East India Company was set up to try and capitalise on this trade. James I granted the company sole rights to trade in India in 1600. This action by the then monarch of England started the special relationship between the private company and the state.

The company fought to establish itself in the region against its Dutch, Portuguese and later French rivals. The path to economic trading was a difficult one. The Dutch had dominance in the spice trade and were loath to give it up. This meant a violent beginning to the company's establishment on the Indian continent. The East India Company decided to settle in the Bay of Bengal and to venture inland for trading options, rather then fight for coastal control.

By 1757, the company had gained significant control in India and a degree of influence in parliament. It had a strong lobbying group that sought to defend the company's interests in parliament. It also had the British Army at its disposal. In 1757, the Battle of Plassey was fought. The unrest was an internal Indian struggle for control of the Kingdom of Bengal. British forces in the service of the East India Company were instructed to intervene. Robert Clive, the commanding officer, led his forces against the reigning ruler of Bengal. Until this point, the kingdom was under control of the Mughal emperor who afforded the company protection and trading rights. The emperors used viceroys as their agents in the region, but Clive's intervention succeeded in establishing Mir Jaffar as the new ruler.

This action ensured that the company's trading activities would be protected. The company was appointed as the region's tax collector in 1765, further establishing itself in the ruling of Bengal. Richard Allen points out that the Battle of Plassey was doubly important "not only because it enabled the British to establish themselves in India but because it established a model for their takeover – a mixture of military conquest and insinuating themselves into the local Indian governments" (Allen, 2000, p. 30). This mixture can be seen quite well in the film *Lagaan* (2001) as the local Indian ruler is beholden to the British to protect him from his neighbouring indigenous rulers.

The Crown, however, did see problems in the East India Company, not least the corruption within it. To combat this, the Crown exercised its right to take a controlling interest in the company. This effectively created a semi-state body with a private element (the shareholders) and a public element (the Crown's control). The national control was governed by the company's board of directors, which now included the

Secretary of State and the Chancellor of the Exchequer. With this degree of state control, Britain could use the company to effectively take control in India.

The East India Company established British power in India during this time using the Supreme Council as the decision-making forum for the country with the Governor General overseeing the process. The Crown appointed these positions on recommendations from government, thus ensuring that the government always had a significant presence in the day-to-day running of British India.

The 1857 Indian Army Mutiny

The British government created a semi-state body because it was reluctant to commit to the ownership of India. It was entrenched in several battles around the globe. It fought and lost a war of independence in North America, which prompted a rebellion in Ireland in 1798. It was also fighting a particularly lengthy war with France, which spilled over into India as the French tried to usurp English control there. But all of that changed in 1857 with the Indian Army Mutiny.

Up to this point, the British has succeeded in establishing hegemonic power in India. This was reinforced by the indigenous Indian belief of the superiority of the British colonisers. The population accepted that English values and virtues were superior to their own, especially in relation to government and education. In 1857, however, unrest started to develop. Sepoys, Indian soldiers in the British army, rose up in an act of rebellion against their colonising rulers.

Sometimes referred to as the 1857 War of Independence, the Indian Mutiny was a direct challenge to British rule in India. It was violent and the mutineers directly targeted British settlers. This prompted massively embellished reports in English newspapers who exaggerated the extent of the violence against women and children in general. In most cases the reports sought to further establish the idea of British superiority over the savage indigenous population, particularly by commenting on the rape of white women by the mutineers before they were executed in savage circumstances. *The Illustrated London News* on 8 August 1857 reported that "Little children of one years old were thrown into the air and caught on bayonets" (Allen, 2000, p. 225). It went on to report that at "Raee a wretch seized a lady from Delhi, stripped her, violated her and then murdered her brutally, first cutting off her breasts" (ibid.).

The mutiny caused uproar at home and it was the East India Company that paid the price for the rebellion. On 2nd October 1858, Queen Victoria signed the act to transfer administration from the East India Company to the crown. This acted as the pathway for Victoria declaring herself Empress of India and the creation of the Raj. British rule in India remained in the hands of the Crown until the granting of independence and its implementation in 1947.

Education and language

The success of the colonisation of India by Britain rested on the colonisers' ability to establish their culture and way of life as fundamentally superior to that of the indigenous populations. In India, as in other territories, this was effected through the education system. The principal aim of a coloniser is to establish their language as the primary one. The British had excellent practice at this, considering that they had all but eradicated the Irish language in Ireland during the same period by means of the education system and trade. School children in Ireland were caned if they spoke in their native tongue. This meant the death of the language at a root level and, since it was fundamentally a language passed on verbally rather then through literature, it was easily marginalised.

In India it wasn't so easy. There was firstly an array of languages and some primary ones. These languages also had written and oral traditions. It became important to devalue these languages and to establish English as the primary language of the land. An action such as this is the mainstay of a colonising country. Language is a fundamental indicator of nationality and nationhood; its removal or devaluation is a significant act designed to further subvert indigenous national identities. Thomas Babington Macaulay made it his goal to establish English as the primary language of British India.

In his *Minute on Education* in 1835, Macaulay was trying to ensure that English was the main language of the education system. His arguments for this were entirely jingoistic in nature. One of the best examples is when he says:

> I have no knowledge of either Sanscrit or Arabic. But I have done what I could to form a correct estimate of their value. I have read translations of the most celebrated Arabic and Sanscrit works. I have conversed, both here and at home, with men distinguished by their proficiency in the Eastern tongues. I am quite ready to take the oriental learning at the value of the orientalists themselves. I have never found one among them who could deny that a single shelf of a good European library was worth the whole native literature of India and Arabia. (In Allen, 2000, pp. 198-199)

Macaulay's sheer disdain and lack of understanding for anything other than traditional European literature exemplifies the separation that existed between the two nations of

India and Britain. But English did become the language of commerce and civil law. The establishment of a canon of English texts to be taught at schools prepared Indian men for a prestigious and valuable career in The East India Company and later the British Civil Service in India.

"In India, English is the language spoken by the ruling class. It is spoken by the higher class of natives at the seats of government. It is likely to become the language of commerce throughout the seas of the East" (in Allen, 2000, p. 199). As Macaulay predicted in 1835, today English is without doubt the language of commerce on the subcontinent, with Indian graduates working in the call centres that service the financial institutions of the UK. But the most telling remark here is the reference to the "ruling class". This statement, twenty-two years before the mutiny and the establishment of the Raj, shows the belief that the British had in their absolute ownership of India.

The rise of Gandhi and Satyagraha

The turn of the 20th century saw a shift in the indigenous feelings in India. There was a vocal and militant side developing, which was in open conflict with the ruling British forces and the Indian plantation owners who supported the British to keep their workforces in check. This revolt was further complicated by the increase in tensions between Muslim and Hindu Indians, and between the Sikh and Tamil population. The India of EM Forster's *A Passage to India* (1924) encapsulates this slide into unrest, which never fully escalated into an outright rebellion, yet was a volatile powder keg.

In *A Passage to India*, the character of Dr Aziz is arrested and tried for the attempted rape of a young, impressionable woman, Ms Quicksted. The ensuing social outfall written by Forster, mirrored the feelings of that period.

But while there is a great knowledge of *A Passage to India* worldwide, whether it is because of the book or the David Lean film of 1984, there is little awareness of Raja Rao's *Kanthapura* (1938). This novel encapsulates the feelings of the ordinary villager during the rise of Gandhi's National Congress and the growth of a policy of non-violent aggression. But it also highlights the impact of British rule on the poorest of Indians:

> ...Millions and millions of yards of foreign cloth come to this country, and everything foreign makes us poor and pollutes us. To wear cloth spun and woven with your own God-given hands is sacred, says the Mahatma. And it gives work to the workless, and work to the lazy. And if you don't need the cloth, sister – well, you can say, "Give it away to the poor," and we will give it to the poor. Our country is being bled to death by foreigners. We have to protect our Mother. (Raja, 1989, p. 17)

Kanthapura is an excellent contemporaneous text that really communicates the idea of 'Satyagraha' or passive resistance. This was the term that Gandhi used to explain the nature of the National Congress. In his essay from September 1917, Gandhi says that "Satyagraha is not a physical force. A Satyagrahi does not inflict pain on the adversary; he does not seek his destruction. A Satyagrahi never resorts to fire arms. In the use of Satyagraha, there is no ill will whatever" (Allen, 2000, p. 300). This non-physical means of protest can be seen in the film *Lagaan*, which we will look at in more detail later. But it is also highlighted in many other texts, simply because it is so spiritual in its definition and spirituality is a particular quality of Indian Bollywood cinema.

It would be unfair not to also discuss Gandhi's anti-Western sentiment. It is without doubt that he sought a peaceful resolution to India's situation, but he was not afraid to lay the blame at the feet of his British rulers. He says in the same 1917 essay that: "Deluded by modern Western civilisation, we have forgotten our ancient civilisation and worship the might of arms." The meaning of this would span the eighty two years between Macaulay's *Minute on Education* and the rise of national unrest. The delusions were that Indians could never be the ruling classes. Even with all of the refinements of British culture now coursing through Indian society, they would never truly be accepted as equal. The lack of equality meant that the contamination of Indian culture had been for nothing, and this is what Gandhi sought to oppose.

Independence and partition

While Gandhi struggled to achieve a united India, the Hindu and Muslim factions quarrelled over the creation of Hindustani India and Pakistani India, in essence a homeland for each. Mountbatten, who was sent as the last British Viceroy, had the job of delivering independence to India by 15 August 1947. The racial tensions were intense and both sides had their own militias for pitched and running battles with their religious enemies.

This had been forshadowed as early as 1906 when Gopal Krishna Gokhale delivered a paper to the East India Association. In it he states that: "England will find on her hands before long another Ireland, only many times bigger, in India" (Allen, 2000, p. 289). The links are obvious as are the routes to independence and the subsequent disputed and unfriendly partition of the country. But Gokhale had reservations as to the development of India. He also stated in the same paper that: "an oriental country cannot hope to advance on Western lines, except by cautious and tentative steps. What Japan has been able to achieve in 40 years, India should certainly accomplish in a century" (ibid.). While we know of the massive improvements India has made, they still haven't quite lived up to Gokhale's expectations. But in 1906 he would not have been able to envisage the separation and separatism that engulfed India in the lead-up and aftermath to independence, a topic which is routinely used in Bollywood storylines as we can see from Mani Ratnam's films *Bombay* (1995) and *Dil Sé* (1998).

The Hindu and Muslim conflict

EM Forster made the division between the two largest faiths in India obvious in *A Passage to India*. The differences and conflicts were part of daily life. The uniting bond was the struggle for independence, but once promised the divisions reopened with even greater venom. Gandhi saw himself as a uniting force, and in truth his followers were from both faiths. He said in September 1946 (before independence): "I had taken up the cause of Hindu-Muslim unity long before I joined the congress" (Allen, 2000, p. 308). He explained that a Muslim firm employed him as a barrister in South Africa but his job was to represent the Hindu population.

Gandhi's concerns also extended to the English consideration of partition as a potential solution to the issue of post-independence religious tension. In the same speech he said:

> I appeal to the English not to nurse the thought that they can divide Hindu and Muslim. If they do they will be betraying India and betraying themselves. Hindus and Muslims are born of the same soil. They have the same

blood, eat the same food, drink the same water and speak the same language. (Allen, 2000, p. 309)

Gandhi was passionate about the relationship between the two faiths. He saw their future as the future of India. If they were separated, India surely would be. This dedication to the restoration of positive relations between the two religions was probably a contributing factor in the fanatical Hindu response to Gandhi and his subsequent assassination in 1948 by a radical Hindu.

When Prime Minister Jawaharlal Nehru addressed the Constitute Assembly in New Delhi on 14 August 1947 he spoke of the new freedoms that India could look forward to. On the eve of independence he said: "At the stroke of the midnight hour, when the world sleeps, India will awake to life and freedom" (Allen, 2000, p. 319). The poignant reading of this statement is intensified by the reality of the mass movement of people at the sametime. Hindus flocked from the north to be in the newly created state of India and Muslims raced north to be part of the newly created state of Pakistan.

The sectarianism was intense as the refugees marched to escape the violence that followed them. Even the Indian army was dissolving along religious lines. This is mirrored in the perpetuation of the violence that we see in Mani Ratnam's *Bombay* and the radical terrorist feelings that we witness in Ratnam's separatist love story, *Dil Sé*. Just twenty-four hours later Nehru addressed the nation by radio and spoke of the "privilege" (Allen, 2000, p. 319) that was bestowed upon him to serve India. He described himself as the "first servant of the Indian people" (ibid.) and later he spoke of India "giving her message of peace and freedom to others, then we have to be big ourselves and worthy children of mother India" (Allen, 2000, p. 320). But he stopped short of directly talking about different faiths or mentioning Pakistan at all. He focused on the birth of modern India.

The conflict that has existed between India and Pakistan since independence may have stuttered towards an *entente cordial*. But this has of course been dictated by other foreign circumstances. The issues of world terrorism post 9/11 have had a dramatic effect on the way Pakistan communicates and engages with the West. This is mirrored by the massive economic growth in India. Both countries now have very important reasons to survive side by side. The nuclear proliferation of the two nations also hastened a retreat from military hostilities for both Islamabad and New Delhi. Being a nuclear power brings with it great responsibility that these two young nations have had to learn to deal with. This new-found respect between the countries has been represented in modern films like *Lagaan: Once upon a time in India*. A popular Hindi film with both Hindu and Muslim villagers fighting the British, it shows that the most popular media in India is also contributing its bit towards positive interfaith communication and peace.

Narrative and convention in Indian cinema: The early years

The Indian film industry grew up under the colonial gaze of the British Empire. The fact that it developed as the country was coming around to the idea of home rule and self-government marks a phase that Elleke Boehmer calls "Colonial Literature"(Boehmer, 1995, p. 2). The term can, in this case, be attributed to the film industry in India, as it represents a cultural, textual art form that has grown and developed in a colonial and post-colonial situation. Boehmer says that Colonial Literature "is the more general term. We can take this to mean writing concerned with colonial perceptions and experience written mainly by metropolitans, but also creoles and indigenes during colonial times" (ibid.). The theory fits very well with the development of the industry in and around the metropolitan conurbation of Bombay.

In the late 19th century the Lumière brothers, August and Louis, exhibited their cinematograph in Paris. Following their success, they embarked on a world tour. In July 1896, the cinematograph arrived in imperial Bombay. It was on show at Watson's hotel in the city and advertisements were taken out in local newspapers advertising the exhibition to the local population. The showing of the short films was so successful that the organisers rented a theatre in the city to extend the screenings and it ended up running right up to the monsoon season. The canny use of the poor weather as a way of attracting people allowed the organisers to extend the lease on the theatre and to show new shorts.

Following the success of the film screenings, a new industry, the tented cinema, began to spring up in the early 20th century. The tented cinemas were pioneered by two men,

Jamjetji Maden and Abdulally Esoofally. Both saw the potential in the distribution of cinema, both the films and the equipment. Maden, who initially saw the theatre as a rising art form in India, switched to cinema after he saw it had real potential. These two tent showmen exhibited their shows in parks on the edge of cities and later they began to travel with the tented cinemas. While Esoofally began as a traveller and later settled in Bombay, having traversed South East Asia with his projector and tent, Maden embarked on a tour of Indian cities and even some remote areas. This culture sparked the travelling cinema of the modern era, which still brings the most recent releases to the remote areas of India.

During this colonial period the films being screened were truly international. In *Indian Film*, Barnouw and Krishnaswamy say:

> ...clearly the film scene in India, as in other countries, was at this time extremely international. France, headed by Pathé, was apparently the leading source, but products of the US, Italy, England, Denmark and Germany also competed for a share of the market. (Barnouw, 1980, p. 10)

During the colonial period there is normally an awakening of traditional art forms and language that has been suppressed by the colonial rulers. In Ireland during the 1880s the Celtic Twilight sought to revive the Irish language and its literary form. The Pan Celtic League, and WB Yeats wrote in English but in a very Irish way. In India, Dhundiraj Govind Phalke was doing the same thing. A Sanscrit scholar and a printer, he saw the potential for the retelling of Indian stories by film. He began slowly, due to the lack of funds available to him, but in a short time he managed to raise enough money to film.

It is widely reported that in 1910 during a showing of *The Life of Christ* at the American-Indian Theatre in Bombay, Phalke saw the potential of making similar films but about Indian religious figures like Krishna. In 1912, after a string of short films, he released his first feature *Rajah Harischandra* (*King Harischandra*). This mammoth feature preceded the long feature style and in some ways may account for the extended length of Indian films today. The film, released in 1913, was a huge success and drew massive audiences to the Coronation Cinema in Bombay.

This was a colonial text and marked the blueprint for the other 80 films that he directed between 1912 and 1937. Phalke was directing during the Raj, a time of British control in India. And, like Yeats, he was amalgamating Indian traditions and stories with the Western format of the silent feature film. Barnouw and Krishnaswamy suggest that:

> The audiences attending the Western films at the new cinema palaces paid little attention to Phalke. The English language newspapers hardly noticed him, and Phalke did not advertise in them. He was reaching, almost at once, a different public. To his audience *Rajah Harischandra* and its successors ... were like revelations. To them the inhabitants of the Western films had been interesting but remote... [and] might as well have come from Mars. In the Phalke films the figures of long-told stories took flesh and blood. The impact was overwhelming. (Barnouw, 1980, p. 14)

This was the first stage in the development towards a new cultural identity and artistic movement.

The second stage was the birth of the Indian talkie in 1931. A new narrative approach began a completely new style of film that can be considered the beginnings of a post-colonial style, even though independence was still seventeen years away. A movement towards a new culture was beginning; this is common as countries edge towards independence. The cultural minds tend to look back to the country's traditions, which have been damaged by the colonial rulers. In this case, Indians looked back to their own classical culture to try and create a modern understanding of what it meant to be Indian. The Indian talkie took the musical elements of the popular classical Sanscrit theatre and brought it to the big screen, developing a new narrative form.

The Indian film industry was immensely popular. The silent era provided the perfect platform in a country with twelve major languages (with Hindi being the national language) and twenty minor regional languages, not to mention the regional dialects that are almost languages in themselves. With this division in language across the country, the silent films provided truly inclusive entertainment for audiences. The style was similar to the Western theatre with most having musical accompaniment and the use of narration screens. The silent era also allowed the Western films to compete equally for space.

By the mid-1920s the Indian cinema industry was producing more than a hundred feature films a year - a greater film output to some of the respected Western producers, including those in England and France and also those in the USSR. Then, as now, Hollywood was the major player in world cinema production and by the 1920s the Hollywood studio system was the perfect platform for a successful film industry. It was founded on a few simple premises which ensured its success:

- Contract the actors to the studio.

- Ownership of the studio space and equipment to produce a wide range of different texts.

- The vertical integration of the industry – control of the filming, distribution and exhibition of the texts produced.

The early Indian studios tried to model themselves on this structure. They strove to achieve vertical integration. By the mid-1920s the Calcutta-based Madan Theatre company had become the most powerful chain of exhibition spaces in the country. In an attempt to recreate Hollywood it bought American sound equipment and built a studio in a suburb of Calcutta, called Tollygunge. The obvious similarity between 'Tolly' and 'Holly' of course ensured the coming of 'Tollywood' in relation to the studio.

In 1931, the studio produced India's first talkie, *Alam Ara* (*Beauty of the World*), directed by Ardeshir Irani. It is a landmark film not only because it is recognised as the first sound film produced in India, but also because it can be credited with being the first of what has become known as the popular Hindi film. Irani realised the importance of music in Indian popular entertainment. He used the basic structure of Parsee theatre, which featured music as an interlude as well as for song and dance sequences. In order to make sure that he got the narrative structure and the use of songs correct, Irani enlisted the help of music composer Ferozshah M Mistri. This partnership ensured that the style of Hindustani popular music that accompanied the parsee theatre plays would also be the music to accompany his films.

Mehboob Khan and *Mother India*

In the chapters that follow I aim to give a range of background information that will assist in the study of Bollywood, even if it is only from the 1990s onwards. I have highlighted important actors, directors and producers and arranged them chronologically; I have also ensured that their careers overlap as much as possible. This helps in the identification of the subtle shifts in the generic formulas of Bollywood. Mehboob Khan is the starting point, as he was one of the first popular Hindi film-makers to successfully take his work to the West. His seminal text, *Mother India* (1957), is still a favourite in India today, even with cross-generational audiences. The film also marked the end of sync sound in Bollywood film-making, which allowed the current Bollywood model to really emerge.

Few films are as revered in Bollywood history as *Mother India*. This simple tale tells the story of Radha's life in a poor village and has continually captured the hearts of the Indian cinema-going public. The film's narrative is a simple *masala* mix of music, romance and honour. The film was the product of one of India's most celebrated producer directors, Mehboob Khan, a genuine self-made man.

Khan's life reads, like many in Bollywood, like a classic Hollywood 'rags to riches' tale. He was born and raised in a remote village called Billimoria, which became the village used in *Mother India*. He was a devout Muslim and always made time for prayer. When he finally opened his own studios, God featured prominently in his mind. While MGM had the roaring lion, Khan had a 'voice of God' narration stating: "Muddai laakh bura chaahe to kyaa hotaa hai, vahi hotaa hai jo manzur-e-Khuda hotaa hai", which translates to: "No matter if the plaintiff wishes you a hundred ills, it is Allah's will alone that determines what befalls you".

He dreamt of becoming a great actor and when he was about sixteen, he ran away to Bombay, hoping to make a name for himself at the great Imperial Studios. His father is reputed to have dragged him home and the poorly educated but defiant and eager Khan became a husband and a father. Even then, he was determined to make it in the movies and so ran away again.

This time he had more luck. He managed to secure a role in a silent feature, *Ali Baba and the Forty Thieves*. As with so much of Bollywood's history there is contention over the date of this film. Mihir Bose, in his book *Bollywood: A History*, and Uperstall.com both maintain it to be 1927. Nasreen Munni Kabir in her book *Bollywood The Indian Cinema Story* states it was called *Ali Baba aur Chalis Chor* and released in 1932, directed by JJ Madden. IMDB doesn't even credit Khan with a performance in a film relating to this title. If the date and title are in doubt, the role he played is not. Khan famously played one of the forty thieves and his job was to hide in a wooden vat.

Even with such austere beginnings, Khan still dreamt of acting fame. But his big break was to come from the other side of the camera. In 1934, having transferred to Sagar Studios, he got the opportunity to direct. The film was called *Al Hilal* (*The Judgement of Allah*), a tale of conflict between Roman civilisation and the emerging Muslim kingdoms that the Romans sought to rule, based on the 1932 Cecil B DeMille film, *The Sign of the Cross*.

This concept of conflict and survival was a continual theme that Khan came back to time and again. This was clearly visible in the 1940 film *Aurat* (*Woman*). It told the tale of a simple village woman who sets out upon a life that becomes fraught with insurmountable struggles and challenges to her honour, which she strives to protect in the face of the intolerable hardship and the final act of having to kill her youngest son to protect both the village's and her own honour. This text is unmistakably influenced by Khan's growing interest in socialist ways of seeing the world, rather than the prevalent capitalist model. The source of his inspiration for this text is another point of contention. Bose states that the inspiration came from the 1931 novel *The Good Earth* by American author Pearl S Buck. He suggests that: "Babubhai Metha, unlike Mehboob, was a well-read man. Metha told Mehboob to consider another Buck novel *The Mother*, which dealt with the life of a Chinese woman" (Bose, 2006, p. 193). Kabir, however, suggests that it wasn't Buck's 1933 novel *The Mother* but Maxim Gorky's 1907 novel *Mother* (Kabir, 2001, p. 126).

Irrespective of the source of inspiration, the film was made by The National Studios as Sagar Studios had collapsed by this time. Interestingly, the purists of Bollywood cinema prefer the humility of *Aurat*, rather than the melodrama of *Mother India*. But it was not *Aurat* that captured the hearts of the Indian cinema-going public but *Mother India*, which was made by Khan's own studios.

His final film before leaving the National Studio in 1942 was *Roti* (*The Bread*).This anti-capitalist tale of a fictional country where the population is split between the city dwellers and the village tribes highlights Khan's growing socialist feelings. As a progression from *Aurat*, *Roti* is a film whose narrative is bulging with the sentiment that money and wealth are socially worthless. The character Seth Laxmidas is a rich city dweller, who dies from lack of water while his car is full of gold. The main reason for his death is the lack of understanding between the rich and the poor. The rich use currency to purchase goods while the tribal villagers use a barter system. Laxmidas, played by Chandra Mohan, is a victim of the bourgeoisie not understanding the proletariat; as a capitalist he simply didn't understand that his gold was worthless to them.

The obvious socialist overtones in Khan's work were compounded by the hammer and sickle motif he chose for his new studio in 1943. Mehboob Studios had the look of an ideologically socialist studio and his previous work in *Aurat* and *Roti* especially seemed to endorse this supposition. But Khan was defiant in his denials:

> I took the hammer and sickle as our symbol because we considered ourselves workers and not just producers, directors and stars. I have been accused of being a communist for using this symbol, but those who know me well know I am no communist. (Kabir, 2001, p. 127)

Whatever Khan's political persuasion, he is credited for creating one of India's most loved films, and one which narrowly missed out on securing an Oscar for best foreign film in 1958. *Mother India* was a project that seems epic in proportion even to modern films. The release of the print took so long that, in the meantime, its star Nargis was able to star in *Miss India* (1957), which was released in March 1957, a full eight months before Khan finally premiered *Mother India* on 25 October 1957.

In some ways it could be argued that Khan was lucky to even complete the project. *Mother India* was fraught with difficulties, which ranged from casting, the procurement of the filmstock, legal battles, the colour process, the censors and even the title. At the Muharat ceremony before the start of the production process, Khan had originally given the film the working title of *This Land is Mine*, an innocuous title that would have avoided any sort of offence to the Indian population. But the final title *Mother India* proved an altogether difficult pill for many to swallow. The reasons for people's displeasure stems from a 1927 book called *Mother India*, written by American author Katherine Mayo. Its text stills arouses a sting of nationalism in modern India's nationalist circles.

Mayo, a historian, wrote the book as a window onto India. She focused her energies on outlining why the Indian people were not fit to self rule at that time. Its publication during this period of heightened nationalism suggested collusion with the British. But Mayo maintained her stance that she received no help from the authorities. Amardeep Singh of Lehigh University states that evidence has now come to light which shows that Mayo *had* been working with the British CID in India, all of which points to the text being a tool of Raj propaganda.

Khan had to work very hard to convince the authorities that the film would depict the real India and not the India depicted by Mayo. At the outset of the preproduction phase he had to seek special permission to import enough film stock to make one hundred and eighty prints of the final film - the average film had about sixty. The main reason for the embargo of large imports was the fragile economic state of the new India; such a large import could have had an impact on the weak foreign exchange reserves of the country.

With film stock for the prints secured, Khan then faced legal challenges from The National Studio. It had produced *Aurat*, the blueprint for *Mother India*, and felt it was a clear breech of copyright. Khan argued that *Mother India* was a new text, with a new script. The two sides settled out of court and Khan carried on the production.

On completion he knew that the colour would be an issue. This was an early period of mass production in colour film and Mehboob knew it had to be of good quality. He chose Gevacolour initially, intending to then blow it up to Technicolor in London. This was a process that he had trialled in 1952 with *Aan* (*Savage Princess*). The only difference was that this time Khan had to personally ensure the success of the print, which meant travelling to London with his master print to supervise the work.

Indian censors are famously prudish, and during the 1950s cinema was becoming the cultural form that puritans and politicians alike chose to denigrate. Mindful of social unrest and potentially offensive scenes, the censors were very picky in the cuts they insisted on. One of the characters in the film is a money-lender, Sukhilala, played by Kanhaiyalal who also performed as the same character in *Aurat* and again in SS Balan's 1967 remake of *Aurat*. He can be seen to be the archetypical evil capitalist in the film, perhaps continuing the idea that was seen in *Roti*. The censors realised the provocative nature of this character. Sukhilala was of course Khan's capitalist trying to scupper the socialist collectivism of the villagers. The censors considered one scene where he taunts Radha (Nargis) too cruel. Another, when he refuses to help the flooded villagers, was considered too challenging for the audience. It is odd, then, that the censors allowed Khan to continually allow Sukhilala to permit sexual favours as a payment option for Radha for the money he had lent her. The censors clearly saw this provocative storyline as less inflammatory than scenes of the propagation of poverty in the newly-independent India.

Mother India is a film steeped in Khan's socialist vision of the way India should be. It begins with Radha kneeling down and kissing the earth of her village in the new mechanised world of 1957 post-independence India. There are a range of montage of shots to create the story of a new waterway under construction. This civilised development has resonances later in the flashback narrative of the film, when the village is flooded. The industrial progress of the country has not only nationalist overtones but also harks back to the Soviet propaganda films of the 1920s and 1930s when the public were informed of the supposed developing greatness of their country.

This new India is of course the juxtaposition of the agricultural India that we see Radha struggle to survive later in the film. We see her being brought back to her homestead and approached by a delegation headed by her son, who asks her to open the new waterway. She initially refuses but then relents and is brought to the ceremony. It is at this point that Khan flashes back to the day of Radha's wedding, a lavish affair full of the colour of the processed Technicolor print he used. The actual story begins here in the past.

Soviet mise-en-scène in Mother India

The story is a simple tale of hardship and struggle. Radha's mother-in-law has mortgaged the family farm to pay for the lavish wedding. It quickly becomes apparent to the family that the crop they produce is cut up by the money-lender as payment for the loan and their share is paltry in comparison. The reality of the situation is that they have barely enough to keep them. Radha's husband, Shamu, struggles with the injustice of this situation and tries to fight against it. Shamu represents the proletariat land workers of India. His family remain only one bad harvest away from destitution, a theme that we see again in *Lagaan* almost fifty years later. The portrayal of the character is yet another example of Khan's fundamental belief and appreciation of the socialist dream.

In an attempt to limit the losses to the money-lender, Shamu and Radha (under Radha's insistence) begin to clear the family's uncultivated fields, which are in a poor condition and littered with rocks. Shamu feels he must provide for and protect his growing family and especially his two sons, the placid and intelligent Ramu and the combustible and provocative Birju. The couple working in the fields together in solidarity dominate this part of the film. Khan uses Soviet-style montage editing to show the progression and the dedication of the husband and wife team. He also creates repeated *mise-en-scènes* in which the blocking is reminiscent of the Soviet propaganda photos of workers striving and enjoying their toils.

But, as any good drama dictates, disaster strikes. Shamu's arms are trapped under a large bolder and as a result he loses them completely. The family's proximity to destitution narrows at this moment. Radha simply works on, both in the field on her own and caring for her disabled husband. But Shamu, under duress from the money-lender Sukhilala, leaves the family. The stigma of his injuries is too much for him to bear. Khan deals with this departure with great sympathy and it is immensely touching. It also marks a definite turning point in the film's narrative. Henceforth, the family undergoes incredible hardship.

The family's plight snowballs into despair; the death of the matriarchal grandmother is only the beginning as the family's life is destroyed by the absence of a male role model and the advent of a disastrous flood that destroys the entire village. Khan again lavishes heartache on the audience by killing off Radha's youngest baby in the flood. At the same time Radha has to fight off the sleazy advances of the money-lender. He is arguably the cause of the problems in her life, but he only offers her a sexual solution - she must become his consort to save her children. Radha's character is cemented at this point as she chooses to spurn the advances of Sukhilala and instead ploughs the uncultivated field. This chapter of the film ends with Radha using the hand plough as the rest of the villagers flee the devastation. As she ploughs, her sons join her and as the song begins the scene is transformed into Radha and her two grown boys ploughing together. This flash-forward in time delivers a new chapter in Radha's life, with Birju and Sukhilala as the main protagonists.

The film changes dramatically here, as it struggles to represent the quest for independence and the battle against injustice that prevails in the village, a metaphor for the workers' struggle against the tyrannical ruler. When Karl Marx called for the workers to revolt, he suggested that this must be an armed struggle. Birju is the one truly Marxist character in the film. In this chapter, Radha tries to marry off both her sons, but the troublesome Birju is refused a match with the village school teacher's daughter. This, and the pressure of Birju's own feelings of isolation and detachment, force him to act in violent and unpredictable ways.

One of the most memorable scenes is when Radha chases the wounded Birju into the burning haystacks. This was dangerous to film and a dangerous scene socially. One of the most famous stories to emerge from the making of *Mother India* was the start of one of India's greatest interreligious marriages. Nargis and Sunil Duit (who plays Birju) fell madly in love off set. Nargis was the most famous Islamic actress and he was the rising Hindu bad boy of Bollywood. To make matters worse, they were playing mother and son, a fact that some audience members found very hard to separate from real life. In the burning haystacks scene, Nargis did suffer burns during filming, but it is the embrace in the scene that really caused the stir, for the passion is obvious.

The film of course ends as a perfect Shakespearian tragedy. The exiled Birju returns with his band of outlaws to take revenge and to take Sukhilala's daughter as his prize. The use of Birju as the classic anti-hero allows a strong Western link to the characters' attributes. At times he is Hamlet, at others Othello, struggling between passion, revenge and finally madness. The final scenes of the flashback are dominated by the power struggle between Radha and Birju. Radha cannot allow him to undermine the village and the traditional ways again. The kidnapping of Sukhilala's daughter is a bridge too far for even Radha, who is the only one with the strength and conviction to stop Birju. She shoots him in the back as he tries to escape. While unexpected and wildly melodramatic, such action shows a depth of character and narrative construction that many Hollywood movies lack the bravery to commit to.

On exiting the flashback Khan juxtaposes the blood of Birju with the flowing of the water through the new water gates. The use of the water is of course highly symbolic of the flood that caused the death of Radha's baby, and the irrigation that it will provide will mean that the land will never again be as arid and barren as the land that took her husband from her. But the strongest symbolism is reserved for Khan's nod to collectivism and industrial development in the new and emerging independent India.

Starstruck: The Rise of Raj Kapoor

Kapoor as the Chaplinesque 'Vagabond' in Awara

It is very difficult to reconcile the immense popularity of Indian stars to the Western psyche. Of course the cult of celebrity is alive and well in Western culture and as a population we crave information, gossip and paparazzi pictures of our favourite stars. But in India this obsession is on a different level entirely. While we want access and information, Indian audiences revere and worship Bollywood stars, treating them more like deities than actors. There have been many mega stars in Bollywood, both past and present. The *Film Fare* awards archives are a good but not entirely complete indicator of success. During the rest of this book we will come into chronological contact with many more stars, but this chapter is reserved for Raj Kapoor.

Kapoor's importance to the evolution of Indian cinema cannot be underestimated. He was the second member of his family to enter Bombay's tinsel town industry, but he spawned a dynasty which is still performing today, most notably for us in the West with his grandson, Anil Kapoor, who plays the underhand host of *Who Wants to be a Millionaire?* in Danny Boyle's *Slumdog Millionaire*. Kapoor was much more than just the grandfather of current stars, he was an icon in his own right. Greatly influenced by Chaplin, he brought an everyman persona to the screen, which appealed to the cinema audience like no other actor before him. In many ways, his successes were necessary for Amitabh Bachchan to become such a superstar that he was known as a one-man industry.

Bose calls Kapoor "The great Indian showman" (Bose, 2006, p. 172), a title which is truly fitting for one of India's most celebrated actors, directors, studio owners and lovers. Kapoor was born into the world of cinema, he didn't just arrive. His path was certainly eased by for him by the success of his father, Prithviraj Kapoor. This immediately separates him from the rags to riches tale of other great directors and studio owners, like Khan. But Kapoor, family association aside, was very much his own man.

Kapoor was born in Peshawar in 1924 to Prithviraj and Ramsarni Kapoor. His father was the son of a police officer, who couldn't understand anyone's wish to become an actor. This was understandable, as Prithviraj had just finished studying at King Edward College in Peshawar and was already in training to become a solicitor. Madhu Jain explains that to Prithviraj's father "actors belonged to the debauched world of wandering street performers nautanki groups (street performers performing folk plays), people outside the pale of society" (Jain, 2005, p. 4). In 1928, when Kapoor was four, his father left for Bombay to become an actor. On arrival the young father tried his luck at the Imperial Studios. After days of queuing he got an extras role in Bhagwati Prasad Mishra's silent film *Do Dhari Talwar* (*Challenge*) in 1929.

Some time later the handsome Prithviraj got the break that every actor dreams of. The heroine of Indian silent cinema, the Jewish actress Ermeline, noticed him as she passed the line of queuing extras. The story goes that Ermeline was so taken aback by his appearance that she insisted on his immediate casting as her husband (the lead role) in the Imperial Studios film *Cinema Girl* (1930). This significant event in Prithviraj's life also proved to be one of the most important in the life of his six-year-old son. This episode was the spark that illuminated the Kapoors as the first dynasty of Indian cinema. Raj's son, Randhir Kapoor once said: "We are like the Corleones in *The Godfather*" (Jain, 2005, p. xxii).

Prithviraj was a socialist and a close friend of Nehru. He saw socialism as a cure to India's difficult cultural situation of an imposed Western system on an Eastern philosophy. He was in many ways a traditionalist. He craved the ability to work on screen and on the stage at the same time. In 1944, Prithviraj set up the Prithvi Theatres. This travelling company brought modern urban Hindi plays to the masses. The company performed 2,662 shows in 5,982 days and Prithviraj played the lead role in every single performance. The Prithvi Theatre plays were more like Western realist theatre than the traditional folk-based Nautanki plays. It was Prithviraj's goal to establish a modern Indian theatre. He was doing this right at the height of his acting career. The closest Western screen icon to Prithviraj is Al Jolson, star of the 1927 talkie *The Jazz Singer*. Just as Jolson was the star of the first Hollywood talkie, Prithviraj was the star of India's first talkie, *Alam Ara*, in 1931. Jolson was a Broadway vaudeville star who hit the big time with *The Jazz Singer*, but this was the zenith of his screen fame. While Jolson worked all through the 1930s and entertained the troops during the Second World War, he never recaptured the limelight. Prithviraj, on the other hand, never lost it. In fact India's first talkie hero is still at the heart of Indian cinema today as his family live on in Bollywood's hall of fame. In 1978, the Prithvi Theatre was re-established under the auspices of the Prithviraj Kapoor Foundation in order to continue his work.

Kapoor Jr. began his acting career with his father in the New Theatre's production of a Debaki Bose film in 1935. But acting was not the young boy's first career choice. He dreamt of becoming an Admiral in the navy, but fate worked against him. As a child he was desperately overweight and suffered the humiliation of the jibs and insults from his peer group. Kapoor said of this period: "I was a fatty... my childhood days were quite miserable" (Bose, 2006, p. 172). But it was through this adversity that Kapoor became, as he called himself, "a joker". He chose to turn the humour onto himself and in so doing took control of the humiliation. He said he was "seeking that which every schoolboy seeks, the love, affection and esteem of others, I wanted to be liked" (Bose, 2006, p. 173).

Kapoor didn't excel at school, and just like his father had a tendency to fail exams. Prithviraj failed his first year law exams while his son failed to matriculate and to get into the cadet school and, subsequently, the navy. Prithviraj actually wanted Raj to pursue a career outside of the cinema, however, Kapoor was bitten by the bug and in love with film. Prithviraj nonetheless insisted that his son learn through the "University of Life" and he didn't make things easy. He feared that his son would only be a child star and he also wanted him to fully understand the business, on screen, behind the camera and in the theatre.

Kapoor started in the studio and the Prithvi Theatres with his father. He undertook all the lowest jobs: assistant roles, trolley puller, clapper boy, even clearing up and sweeping up the cuttings in the editing department. But he was hard working and managed to become third assistant director for Kadir Sharma. He studio hopped from Ranjit Studios to Bombay Talkies, all the while still working as an assistant in the Prithvi Theatres. It was while working for Sharma in 1947 on the film *Vish Kayna* (*Poison Girl*) that he got his big break, even if it occurred in unusual circumstances. Unable to restrain his still sometimes foolish behaviour, Kapoor always insisted on combing his hair before the clapper was clapped to mark the shot. The only problem was that he was the clapper boy and his actions, while humorous to the crew, were a waste of time. Unfortunately for Kapoor, during the filming of a particular scene, Sharma instructed him not to comb his hair because of the extremely tight time constrains on the crew, to capture the shot before the light was gone. Kapoor ignored him, and combed his hair, catching the lead actor's fake beard in the action and pulling it off. The shot was lost, the light gone and Sharma was furious. He slapped Kapoor across the face in front of the entire crew, bruising his face badly, before throwing him off set.

Interestingly, and for reasons that are still not really known, shortly after this event Sharma called Kapoor to his office to reconcile their differences. Jain quotes Sharma as saying: "The next morning I felt bad and I gave him a contract promising him the role of a hero in my next film, *Neel Kamal*"(Bose, 2006, p. 174). As a result, 1947 became a landmark year for Kapoor in many ways. It was the year of Indian independence and it was the year that *Shakuntala* became the first Indian film to be shown in the US.

In 1947, the young Kapoor starred in *Chittir Vijay* (*The Victory Over Chittor*), *Dil Ki Rani* (*Sweetheart*) and *Jail Yatra*, while still keeping busy at the Prithvi Theatres. A year later in 1948, he left the Prithvi Theatres to set up RK Studios. Kapoor was very intelligent in his preparation for the formation of RK Studios. He and his family got by on some of his earnings from film and his theatre work so that he could finance the studio and, more importantly, finance *Aag* (1948).

It has been suggested that *Aag* (meaning 'fire') drew on the life of Kapoor's father. The story is based around a theatre producer, the three women in his life and his need to find love. The story is told in flashback, an unusual device for a Bollywood film. The film almost cost Kapoor everything. He had remortgaged all that he owned to pay for it and when it was finished he needed it distributed, fast. He did initially struggle to shift the print, but once he found a distributor the film ran for 16 weeks. Kapoor was creating a style all of his own, but the success of *Aag* also provided the financial backing for the film which truly launched him as a director.

On 21 April 1949, Kapoor released *Barsaat* (*Rain*), a film that predominantly dealt with love and people's attitudes to love. One character, Gopal, is a roughish lover, with many alluded conquests, while Pran (Kapoor) is seeking Mrs Right. It is Gopal's character that is at odds with the traditional values of the Hindi society. Kapoor's casting of Nargis was a crucial decision. She had moved on with him from *Aag*, proving her trust in him. But there was also their longstanding and secret romance that flourished until she jumped ship to star in *Mother India*. In India, Nargis was becoming famous for playing amazingly modern characters and "yet in the end reassuringly traditional" (Bose, 2006, p. 177) roles.

Kapoor's career went from strength to strength; his strong directorial style mixed with some shrewd business decisions helped him and RK Films progress quickly. When he chose Nargis to be his leading lady he was taking a risk. In Nargis, Raj was getting a talented actress, an intelligent, modern woman and a beautiful heroine. But Kapoor was also getting a leading lady who was far from an accomplished singer. The biggest actress and singer at the time was Suraiya, with 46 staring roles between 1941 and 1950 and more than 25 playback singer credits in the same period. Bose tells us:

By 1948/9, Suraiya was the highest-paid female star of her time. She was generating the sort of hysteria comparable only to Rajesh Khana in the late 1960s and early 1970s. Shop keepers would draw down their shutters just to see her films on the first day of their release. (Bose, 2006, p. 175)

However great her fame, Suraiya was surpassed by Nargis and the rise of the playback singer. The playback style of Bombay film song didn't really become a wholesale industry device until 1950. This new singing vogue released Nargis from the constraints of being an ordinary singer. Suraiya faded out of the business, completing her final film, *Rustom Sohrab*, in 1963. She died in her Marine Drive apartment in Bombay in 2004.

Playback singers are a generic convention, fully accepted in Bollywood. Once the industry moved away from sync sound after *Mother India*, the pressure on actors and actresses to be accomplished singers was removed. This is in contrast to the Western film form where we expect the actors purporting to sing to actually be the singers of the song. In present day India, the audience would already know who sang the songs before they saw the film. The soundtracks would already have been on sale, with the stars on the cover but the playback singers' names on the CD. The playback singers of Bollywood are stars in their own right, and in many ways they can help make or break a film. But when they first emerged in the 1930s their roles were just as clandestine as the playback singers of Hollywood. Producers didn't want to devalue the star of their film.

Kabir suggests that the introduction of the playback singer allowed the industry to grow and seek new talent:

Once the playback singers arrived on the scene, thereby freeing the screen talent from the need to be able to sing themselves, the casting widened and a new group of stars emerged, approaching film acting in quite a different way from the stage actors of previous years. (Kabir, 2001, pp. 161-162)

Lata Mangeshkar is possibly the most well-known singer in India as a result of her playback career. She is credited as being the backing singer on 1,093 films between 1942 and 2007. She has worked with all the best actors, directors and producers in the history of Bollywood and is an icon of the Indian cinema, or at least her voice is. But she did have to fight for recognition and she didn't get her first screen credit until Kapoor's *Barsaat* in 1949. It is worth mentioning here that IMDb.com does still list her as uncredited in *Barsaat*. She is, however, fully credited in the *Guinness Book of Records* as being the world's most recorded singer, performing more than 25,000 songs. Mangeshkar is, unsurprisingly, the voice of the female lead in many of the films in this book, including *Mother India*, *Sholay*, *Amar*, *Akbar*, *Anthony*, *Dil Sè*, *Lagaan* and *K3G*.

Nargis was more to Kapoor than just his leading lady. He once said: "Nargis was my inspiration, meri sphoortti (my energy). Women have always meant a lot in my life, but Nargis meant more then anyone else" (Bose, 2006, p. 178). One of the reasons was that Nargis regularly invested her own money in Kapoor's films, without which he couldn't have made many of them. The other very well-publicised reason for Kapoor's affection for Nargis was that he loved her. They carried on a secret (or not so secret depending on the different biographical sources) love affair from the late 1940s until the mid-1950s until an acrimonious split and Nargis's subsequent marriage to *Mother India* co-star Sunil Dutt. On a Bollywood delegation to the USSR in 1954 Kapoor and Nargis were said to be like a married couple, reportedly even sharing a hotel room. And on an Indian trade delegation to the US in 1956 they were photographed holding hands together near President Truman.

This deep affection worked both ways. Nargis felt valued and respected by Kapoor. She was allowed to voice her opinions and pitch ideas that ended up in the final prints of the films they made together. This coming together was as romantic as the films they made, but unlike the normal Bollywood film plot Kapoor didn't get the girl.

Arguably, Kapoor's finest hour came in 1951 with the release of *Awara* (*Vagabond*)'. *Awara* was a hit for Kapoor and not just in India but all over the Eastern world, including Turkey and the USSR. It was Kapoor's first inception of his everyman character that would make him a superstar, and would be seen again in *Shree 420* (*Mr 420*) in 1955 and *Bobby* in 1973.

Awara is a complicated tale of modern contemporaneous post-independence India. The plot is contrived around a rather formulaic mix-up. Leela Raghunath (Leela Chintis) is an honourable wife to Justice Raghunath (Prithviraj Kapoor). When Leela falls pregnant, Justice Raghunath is led to believe it is another man's child and throws his pregnant wife and unborn child out on the street. The now illegitimate son, Raju (Raj Kapoor), grows up a vagabond (Awara), living on the streets. Raju turns to crime as a means of supporting his now ill mother. He becomes tied up in a street gang run by Jagga (KN Singh). It turns out that Jagga is more than just the gang boss. Several years before he had been convicted of a crime he didn't commit by Justice Raghunath and to gain revenge he conspired to create the situation that culminated in Leela being thrown out of her home for her presumed infidelity. On discovering this Raju kills Jagga and also tries to kill who he now knows is his father, the judge.

The film is told in flashback as Rita (Nargis) tries to defend Raju in court. The formulaic, almost Shakespearian plot was well received by the audience who adored the slow revealing tension of the flashbacks. Another moment of audience reception that caused a storm was a scene showing Nargis in a swimsuit, which as Jha says was "for a mating game played out at a scale hitherto unknown to Hindi cinema" (Jha, 2005, p. 10).

Kapoor was not afraid to deal with erotic scenes and as director of *Satyam Shivam Sundaram* (*Love Sublime*, 1978), he again pushed the boundaries of exposed flesh. In the film he exploited the free spirit and the willingness of Zeenat Anam in order to show more flesh on screen. He famously said: "Let people come to see Zeenat's tits, and they'll go out remembering the film" (Bose, 2006, p. 304). But although he was content, he faced fierce criticism from some members of the public and the industry, including his preferred playback singer, Lata Mangeshkar.

Awara allowed Kapoor to explore his idea of "an idealist, Chaplinesque common man" (Thompson & Boardwell, 2003, p. 409). In fact, Kapoor was obsessed with Chaplin and the Hollywood greats of his period. While his early films *Aag* and *Barsaat* were influenced by the Italian Neo-Realist film-makers of post-war Europe, his later films were influenced by his feelings on the socialist stigma of the haves and the have nots. In some ways he was appealing to the lowest common denominator of the greater Indian film-going audience, saying: "My fans are the street urchins, the lame, the blind, the maimed, the have nots and the underdog" (Thompson, 2003, p. 409).

Kapoor looked to inspire optimism for the populist audience through his films. He saw Frank Capra's 1934 film *It Happened One Night* as a key film and it led him to try and champion the underdog. His love of Chaplin dovetails into his overarching philosophy. As Bose states: "[Chaplin] was his mentor for *Awara* and all his other films" (Bose, 2006, p. 178).

The success of *Awara* is significant as it had massively important international appeal, especially in the USSR. While Kapoor, like Khan, always denied any communist sympathies, the script was penned by the Marxist writer Khwaja Ahmed Abbas. The film was also made at a time when the Indo-American relationship was at a particularly low ebb. Indian films tended to drift east rather than west. In the seminal Indian cinema text, *Indian Film*, Erik Barnouw and S. Krishnaswamy highlight the relationship between the producer director and his choice of scriptwriter: "RK Films attracted the proletarian themes of Abbas" (Barnouw, 1980, p. 159). As Abbas was a Marxist, he intertwined his beliefs into his writing. This allowed Kapoor to connect with the populist audience through Abbas' optimistic ideals.

With the production of this film hegmonically directed in this way it was destined to be a hit in the Soviet countries and it is even reported that a print was flown to the North Pole Soviet expedition in 1954. When Kapoor and Nargis visited the USSR in 1956 they were amazed at the reception. One of the key songs from *Awara* was played at the airport as they arrived. Interestingly, Barnouw and Krishnaswamy claimed that: "A number of Bombay producers subsequently injected 'proletarian' angles into production in the hope of sharing in the Soviet windfall" (Barnouw, 1980, p. 160). According to Boxofficeindia.com, *Awara* is reported to have made 1,25,00,000 Indian rupees, making it the sixth top earner in the 1950s.

Kapoor's legacy still lives on in Indian cinema today through his extended family. He died in 1988 but *Awara* was remade by Anyat Ullah Khan in 1986, re-stating the longevity of Kapoor's storytelling abilities.

End Notes

1   Note this film is sometimes spell Awaara, however Awara is the spelling used from the original print.

Amitabh Bachchan: Bollywood's greatest survivor

Amitabh Bachchan - Bollywood's biggest star

Kapoor neatly leads us to Bachchan and his rise to fame, his fall from grace and his revival via a TV quiz show and savvy movie choices in the noughties. This chapter is primarily concerned with arguably the most successful Bollywood film of all time, *Sholay* (*Flames*), and how it managed to redefine the Bollywood structure.

Amitabh Bachchan is not your regular formulaic Indian superstar; he is too tall and gangly and his sallow skin gives him a Latin or Mediterranean appearance. He comes from a family of poets and not from an Indian acting or production dynasty. But Bachchan is a superstar of global proportions: "He was voted star of the millennium on a BBC online poll, beating actors like Lawrence Olivier, Marlon Brando and Humphrey Bogart... a statue of Bachchan was installed in Madam Tussards Wax Museum in 2000" (Ganti, 2004, p. 121).

Bachchan's life in the movies hasn't been perfect and in studying him we can enjoy a story which is as marketable as any of the Bollywood features. The young man was convinced he was destined to be an actor, but like any modern great he had to work his way through a variety of meaningless jobs before he got his break. The son of the accomplished poet and academic Harivansh Rai Bachchan, he was born in Allahbad. At the time his father taught English at Allahbad University and his mother, Teji, was a modern and outspoken woman with an accomplished stage acting career behind her.

The society that he grew up in was in many ways a privileged one. Amitabh's father completed his doctorate at Cambridge and was committed to education, and to Amitabh's education. He attended boarding school and then went on to complete college. In her book *Amithabh: The Making of a Superstar* Susmita Dasgupta outlines the difficulty that someone from this sort of background had in making a move to film. She writes: "These days there are many that leave their cushy jobs to try their luck in films, but a good 35 years ago it was not really common, especially when Amitabh had no godfather in the film industry" (Dasgupta, 2006, p. 3). Bachchan's cushy job was an executive position in a shipping company in Kolkata.

Bose disagrees with Dasgupta. He suggests that there was already a family relationship that might have helped to influence him towards film as a career. According to Bose, Bachchan's father was a regular audience member at Prithviraj Kapoor's Prithvi Theatre performances. He was also a regular backstage visitor and after-show attendant, where he would "recite his poems, which Prithviraj liked" (Bose, 2006, p. 268).

What is also not in doubt is the closeness of the Bachchan and the Nehru family. The educated, westernised Bachchans were the perfect blend of an Indian traditional family infused with the culture and refined aspects of the British community. This was complimented further by the family's devout nationalist outlook, which was fully realised in the 1980s when Bachchan retired from acting and ran for parliament.

In 1969, he left the shipping business and travelled to Bombay to begin his new career as a Bollywood actor. He, like many others, found that the streets of Bombay were not paved with gold. But he persevered and broke through in 1969 with KA Abbas's *Saat Hindustani* (the known English title is *Seven Indians*). His early career was pretty unsuccessful, with many of his first films considered flops. But among these there were some strong performances and films that have been received far better as they have aged. In 1970, he co-starred in *Anand* with the then God of Indian cinema, Rajesh Khana. Amitabh showed promise in this film, so much so that he won the Filmfare award for Best Supporting Actor.

He first began to see some commercial success in 1972 with the comedy *Bombay to Goa* (1972) By 1973, he had already made 10 films, but with little success. His 14th film, Parhash Mehra's *Zanjeer* (1973), was the text that launched his career on to the path of superstardom and gained him the reputation of the angry young man. In the film, Bachchan was cast as a broody policeman whose parents were killed in front of him, similar to Bruce Wayne in Tim Burton's 1989 *Batman*. Just as Michael Keaton's surly anti-hero redefined the superhero film, Bachchan's cop character did the same for Bollywood. This angry anti-hero appealed to audiences' darker side. These roles also allowed Bachchan to transcend his very un-*masala* mix frame and looks. Bose tells us: "The film would set the pattern for many of Bachchan's movies that followed, and gave the films of the 1970s the convenient short-hand title of the decade of the angry young man" (Bose, 2006, p. 267).

Sholay

One of the most successful Bollywood films of all time was indeed an angry young man film. Ramesh Sippy's 1975 film

Sholay (*Flames*) was the vehicle that finally established Bachchan as the new superstar of Bollywood. Interestingly, Bachchan is arguably not the real star of the film. This buddy movie westernises the narrative of the Bollywood film. *Sholay* has been dubbed the first Curry Western, so-called because of the film's similarities to Hollywood Westerns and the Spaghetti Westerns of Sergio Leone. Sippy was very much inspired by Leone's films, such as the ultra-violent *Once Upon a Time in the West* (1969).

Sholay was a film that redefined the culture of not just Bollywood but of India also. It was rooted principally in the Bollywood traditions but carried huge culturally imperialistic American overtones. The opening shoot-out scene on the train is taken straight out of the Hollywood genre model for success. In many ways, the train scenes in *Indiana Jones and the Last Crusade* (1989) are not totally different, but again the references to *Once Upon a Time in the West* are visible.

The ideology of the train does also have a very special meaning to the Indian cinema audience. To say the train is spiritual in India might be pushing it, and while it is not necessarily sacred, it is certainly cherished and revered. The arrival of a national railroad network to India in the 19th century was an event that altered the cultural landscape in many ways. It opened up the country to travel, allowing people to migrate from the poorest rural areas to the bustling cities. It allowed goods and resources to be transported, bringing essentials to the furthest flung parts of the vast country. It also transported the civil service structure of the Raj, bringing English culture and teachings and the British army to every part of the land.

In her book, *Planet India*, Mira Kamdur reminisces on Indian rail travel when she writes:

Travelling by train in India is a 19th century experience. Gliding on trains laid into vast interiors to bring raw materials to the bustling port cities, the train is a souvenir in steel of the conquest of the earth by industrious Western powers. Jet aircraft take passengers to any city in India within a couple of hours. A train journey takes time, whole days and nights, through a country air passengers never see. By the end of the journey after sharing snacks, watching each others bags during bathroom breaks, learning each others life story and listening to each others snores, parting always provokes a peculiar sadness. (Kamdar, 2007, p. 145)

Kamdur's connection with the train goes some way to explain the reverence towards it in Bollywood films. The train is an important character in *Sholay*, but other Indian directors use the train to convey the realities of life. Ratnam uses it in both *Bombay* and *Dil Sè* and even Ray uses it to great effect in the simplest way in *Pather Panchali*.

In the 1970s, India was still in the grip of an economic disaster named by the government as The Emergency. Imports were tightly controlled and kept to a minimum with embargoes and high duties in place to quell the desire for imported goods and imported inflation. Veeru and Jai, the two main characters of *Sholay*, were denim-clad gangsters who cut a strikingly Western pose. Bose says: "Veeru and Jai emphasise their urban outlook by wearing denim jeans" (Bose, 2006, p. 288). The use of denim allowed Sippy to further highlight his influences from Hollywood's Westerns while remaining contemporary.

The government powers of The Emergency, including the nationalisation of the country's banking system, had a direct impact on Western cultural influences. Hollywood films, for example, were rarely shown in India, and economically India was, as Nehru intended, more socialistic then capitalistic. This led to poor relations with the US, especially as India maintained good relations with the USSR.

Even with the obvious influences on Sippy, the storyline of *Sholay* is a classic revenger's tragedy. This is again where the *Once upon a Time in the West* similarities become intertwined. In *Sholay*, a retired policeman, Thakur Baldev Singh, hires two tough crooks, Veeru and Jai, to capture the evil bandit Gabbar Singh. The simple storyline is embellished by the fact that there is a Bollywood narrative and Bachchan's brooding angry young man persona at work.

Shortly after the story begins we flashback to Veeru and Jai being transported to jail by train, but the train comes under attack from bandits. They prove themselves to be fearless heroes who protect Baldev Singh, their guard. This simple plot device allows the audience to see the underlying moral good in the characters.

The story only took a month to write:

> Salim, Javed and Ramish formed a script writing trio and... developed a story that heavily borrowed from foreign influences such as Akira Kurosawa's *Seven Samurai*, *The Magnificent Seven*, *Butch Cassidy and the Sundance Kid*, and Sergio Leone's Spaghetti Westerns. But to these they added those touches that make popular Hindi cinema so distinctive. If this made it the first truly *masala* Curry Western, it also carried the story forward with a plot that was much tauter than in previous films of this genre. (Bose, 2006, p. 283)

The clever intertwining of Western influences and the *masala* mix of Bollywood engineered a massive hit for the producers.

The film's cast was not predetermined and the ever-developing Bachchan was by no means the first choice to play Jai. His strong debut in *Anand* and his Filmfare award for best newcomer both stood in his favour. But it was his performance in *Bombay to Goa* that showed his versatility and as a result his overall potential. Dharmendra was already an established star and confirmed for the film. Everyone in the industry expected Bachchan's *Bombay to Goa* co-star, Shatrughan Sinha, to take the part of Jai. He was already an accomplished and established star, but more importantly, he was a bankable asset. Hema Malini, another established star completed the cast. But Sippy was afraid of overloading the film with stars, a recent technique which had begun to sour with audiences. Moreover, Dharmendra's lobbying for Bachchan finally paid off. The casting was a surprise not just to Sinha, but to the wider Bollywood community; Sippy was seen to be taking a risk by placing so much on an unproven actor.

Sholay took Sippy two years to shoot. Production began in 1973, shortly after the release of *Zanjeer*. The success of *Zanjeer* immediately confirmed Sippy's astute choice of Bachchan, who was seen in a very different light now by the rest of the industry. *Sholay*, like many Bollywood films, was plagued by problems, some of which Sippy was principally responsible for. Quite early in the film Veeru and Jai share a song titled "Yeh Dosti Hum Nahin Todenge" (This Friendship of Ours will Never Break). In an unashamed tribute to the "Raindrops Keep Falling on My Head" musical scene from *Butch Cassidy and the Sundance Kid*, this scene is played out on a motorbike with a sidecar and Bachchan playing his harmonica (a motif taken directly from *Once Upon a Time in the West*), and serves as an example of extreme male bonding. However, it took Sippy twenty-one days to shoot, adding a significant amount of time to the entire project.

Elements of this film are reminiscent of the well-made Westerns of the 1950s. The long chase and shoot-out scene leading up to Jai's death is a particularly good example of Sippy taking all his Western influences and rolling them into a *masala* mix Curry Western. As Veeru, Basanti and Jai escape from the bandits the landscape and the style of the camera shots mirror those by John Ford. The long shot and the extreme long shot are used to establish distance and pace between the three stages of the chase. Veeru and Basanti ride in front followed by Jai as he tries to catch up and hold off the pursuing bandits. The shoot-out at this point is only between Jai and the bandits, and the audience already feels that this will not go well. The shooting of Jai in the back is another nod to the Western – the good guys would never shoot anyone in the back. When we enter the next phase of the shoot-out, the camera angles shift to medium close-ups and close-ups. Sippy is again directing the audience's tensions to the action and the fate of Jai, who we know is hurt far worse then he allows Veeru to think.

The close violence of the shots is complimented by the quality of the stunts, for the coordinated falls and the general movement of the extras are well designed. Sippy employed Jim Allen, an English stunt coordinator, to try and replicate the Hollywood quality stunts he had seen. However, as Bose tells us, the relationship took a while to gel:

> The English brought gadgets and equipment Bollywood had not seen before: pads for shoulders, ankles, knees and elbows. They also taught the Bollywood stunt people new techniques on how to cushion falls or time jumps. There were also, inevitably, cultural problems. The English were used to a more rigorous method of working. During one scene when Dharmendra had to shoot real bullets, he had gotten drunk... The bullets he fired flew perilously

close to Bachchan. (Bose, 2006, p. 294)

While the teething problems took a while to settle, the finished print shows Allen and his crew's accomplishments. The stunts look far more polished than any in Bollywood before.

Jai's Death in Sholay

The style of the production during Jai's shoot-out scene was devised to look just like a Hollywood Western. Bose again tells us: "Many of the action shots were exact copies of movies such as *Butch Cassidy and the Sundance Kid.*" (ibid.). The shot in which a bandit climbs along the bottom of the bridge is also similar to Charles Bronson's climb across the top of the train in *Once Upon a Time in the West*. It was these shots that exposed the Indian cinema-going public to the conventions that Western audiences had already enjoyed for a considerable amount of time. Sippy's march towards a westernisation of Bollywood has had real and lasting effects, which can be seen in Bollywood texts like *Lagaan*.

When a film takes two years to shoot, life will inevitably get in the way and cause further complications for the director. Sippy had an interesting dual love story while on set. Bachchan and Jaya Bhaduri were very much a couple and very much in love; they had married just before shooting began. They formed a pact while Bachchan was shooting *Zanjeer*; if the film was a success they planned to travel to London to celebrate. They subsequently married and set off on a double celebration - a honeymoon and a successful film release. When they returned they began shooting *Sholay* in October 1973.

Bollywood films, like Hollywood films, are shot in a non-chronological order and one of the first scenes filmed was one in which Radha (Jaya) receives some keys from Jai. But Jaya was now three months pregnant and far plumper than the character profile that was expected. She also suffered from terrible morning sickness. After birth, Jaya remained plump, never really losing the baby weight. Radha's character is bitten by remorse for her murdered husband. She was initially thought to be a character who would be very thin, carrying the outward physical signs of her sorrow. Jaya's pregnancy and post-pregnancy figure were at odds with the idea of the character. However, if Jaya had lost weight after giving birth it would have caused Sippy even more problems. A Radha with a consistent figure would be far better then a Radha whose weight fluctuated wildly on-screen.

Jaya and Amitabh's love story was not the only romance on set. The love story of Dharmendra and Hema Malini, who played the outspoken and vivacious Basanti, is a little like the storyline of the 1981 Karel Reisz film *The French Lieutenant's Woman* in which the on-screen love story is replicated off-screen but with the issue of the actors being married. In the case of *Sholay*, Dharmendra was already married and had no intention of leaving his wife. Nor was Hema single; her long-time suitor, the actor Sanjeev Kumar, had already proposed to her. This, of course, caused problems on set. As Thakur Baldev Singh was played by Kumar he had a particularly important role in the film, acting as the catalyst for Veeru and Jai to go after Gabbar and his goons. But Kumar was not just unhappy in love but in life. He migrated from the stage to film hoping to be a hero character - he wanted to be Veeru. But it was his excellent training and acting skills that actually prevented him from the heroes' roles. If we were to consider Kumar in terms of Hollywood actors, he would be similar to James Wood, William Dafoe or Gary Oldman; a consummate character actor, well-respected and constantly working, but never stereotypically the leading man. This hung heavy on Kumar who found solace in drinking. Sippy was very aware of this and matched his shooting schedule to Kumar's troubles. He drank late into the night and rose late, normally hung over. Sippy therefore ensured that his shots were filmed in the afternoon, giving him time to recover. Upperstall.com remarks of his death: "A bachelor, Sanjeev Kumar died of an acute heart ailment in 1985. It is ironic that someone who had played so many elderly roles, himself didn't even live to be fifty..." ("Sanjeev Kumar | Upperstall.Com," n.d., para. 10). While he died alone, Hema went on to have Dharmendra's children, his second family, and after much turmoil they married in 1980.

Sippy also contrived to make the filming of *Sholay* even more difficult than necessary because of his wish to shoot on 70mm film, rather than the usual 35mm. There were huge issues here, the first being resources. There were no 70mm cameras in India and the cost of importing them was prohibitive. Sippy devised a simple solution - to enlarge the 35mm print to 70mm. His brother Ajit was instructed to carry out tests on the process. Once it was established that the print could be enlarged without losing quality, the decision was finalised that *Sholay* would be a 70mm film.

But Sippy now encountered another problem. There were very few cinemas in India equipped to screen 70mm prints and so he made the fateful decision to produce two negatives, one 35mm print to enlarge to 70mm and one 35mm print for the more general release in India. Two negatives meant that each shot had to be filmed twice. This caused a considerable time delay in production and goes some way to explaining the two-year production schedule. This was not an efficient production cycle for a mainstream Bollywood film and it put considerable pressure on the producers, who now had to hope for a total box-office smash to cover costs.

The Indian censors are notoriously demanding on film-makers. And the censors can be both at a national and a local level, as we will discuss later with Ratnam's *Bombay*. In the case of *Sholay*, the censors had some grave concerns. It was violent, ultra-modern, unashamedly Western in influence and totally irreverent in relation to authority. While they insisted on several cuts the most troubling directive was in relation to the ending of the film. The original print ended with Gabber Sing's head being crushed under Baldev Singh's foot as the army surrounds them from the top of the hills. The censors disliked the constabulary link to Baldev, arguing that as a retired policeman he still embodied the values of the police and by killing Gabber he compromised those values.

The reasons for this censorial directive lay in the social and political climate of the day. India was in the grip of The Emergency, an acute period of time in Indian political and economic history where the country was in serious flux. The already tense Hindu-Muslim relationship was being fractured further as India and Pakistan moved further apart from each other, especially after India's nuclear tests of 1974. The authorities did not want to be seen as condoning violence perpetrated by the military or the police and the censors insisted on a reshoot. Sippy regrouped, reshot and re-edited both the 70mm and the 35mm print.

Sholay's final production problem occurred as the film was to premier. The 70mm print had been finished in a lab in London and had to be returned to India in time for the premier in Bombay. The enlarged 70mm print was in many ways an import and, as a way of controlling the country's economic stability, imports had significant restrictions and duties on them. But as Bose reported, Sippy also thought that a disgruntled politician intervened to try and stop the print being sent to Bombay for the premier.

This implausible conspiracy theory actually appears more likely when you consider the espionage at work in London. Sippy intended and advertised a London premier at the Odeon Marble Arch before they were due to fly back to India. But they were tipped off that a team from the Indian Embassy was instructed to intercept and confiscate the print. Sippy cancelled the screening and flew to India and, as predicted, a team arrived at the cinema ready to seize the print. The flight of the print from the law couldn't last forever and when they landed in Bombay the authorities impounded it. Sippy pulled some of strings and managed to get political allies to intervene and to get the print released, but not in time for the premier. The 70mm print arrived at the cinema just as the 35mm was ending; the decision was made to play the 70mm version straightaway and the premier continued until the small hours.

Life after *Sholay*

Sippy had wagered a lot on *Sholay* but it was not the immediate hit that was predicted. Its audience numbers were good, but the response was decidedly mute. The audience seemed to watch the film in silence. Normally, Indian cinemas are loud and vibrant places as the audience cheers and boos along with the narrative, but the cinema audience at a showing of *Sholay* was different. The critics were divided. There were scornful reports of mimicry in relation to Sippy's homage to the Spaghetti Western, but many reviews seemed to all come to the same conclusion that - this was a very different movie.

Sippy was so worried that he actually called a meeting with the principal cast and crew where he stated that he knew why people were reacting in this unusual manner. The death of Jai was a mistake, in many ways a bridge too far for the audience to suffer. His hypothesis was that the audience had come to love Jai so much that they simply couldn't and therefore wouldn't accept his death. He proposed entirely reshooting the film from the point of Jai's death. It was then that all involved figured the audience response out; it wasn't so much muted as shell-shocked. The audiences, having never experienced anything like it before, simply couldn't express their feelings, but the overall feeling was that they loved it. Most went to see it twice and the film "ran consecutively for five years in Bombay and continues to be re-released to full houses…[it has]…mythical status in the Bombay film industry and among audiences as the pinnacle of film-making" (Ganti, 2004, p. 161).

With *Sholay* a hit, Bachchan now moved on and came under the influence of another director, Manmohan Desai. Desai only directed 20 films, but eight of those featured Bachchan. Desai was perhaps the greatest influence on Bachchan's career post-*Sholay*. The success of *Zanjeer* and *Sholay* established him as part of the new generation of brooding young actors. His characters were non-conformist and disillusioned but with firm morals, similar to Bachchan himself, who was a private person and shunned the mercenary film media. In many ways he cut a similar figure to John Osborne and his angry young men contemporaries of 1950s British theatre. But in the popular world of film, with its high economic pressures, a happy medium needed to be established between this angry character actor and his now adoring public. It was Desai who unlocked the middle ground and transformed Bachchan from a star to a superstar. Susmita Dasgupta notes: "Desai took Amitabh out of the realist cinema and put him in the conventional melodrama" (Dasgupta, 2006, p. 42).

The MKD Productions film *Amar, Akbar, Anthony* (1977) directed by Desai, is the film credited with reinventing Bachchan and propelling him to stellar stardom. The film is convoluted and complicated in its plot design and uses many conventions favoured by Desai during his career. It returned to the multi-star formula that *Sholay* worked so hard to avoid two years before. Amar, Akbar and Anthony were all brothers separated at birth, who find each other as friends before they discover their brotherhood. Desai liked to use similar plot structures such as "mistaken identity, lost and found siblings and highly improbable feats" (Ganti, 2004, p. 103) and they proved successful enough for him to reinvent them in some form in his other films. One of the most important themes of Desai's films and *Amar, Akbar, Anthony* was religious secularism. In the film, each of the brothers is brought up in a different religion: Muslim, Hindu and Catholic. Desai was overt in his representation of India as a country where people could live together regardless of their faith, and Bollywood was a strong vehicle for spreading his belief in secularism.

In Anthony Gonsalves, Bachchan's character in the film, the actor revealed a new persona for his growing fans. A light-hearted and jovial Anthony endeared him to many more adoring followers. The release of *Don* in 1978 saw Bachchan in another mistaken identity storyline with him being asked by the police to pretend to be a dead mafia boss. *Don* was another huge success, making Bachchan the hero of comedy and action movies. He had become the most bankable Bollywood asset and seemingly the most versatile actor in Bombay.

In 1982, he and Sippy made another smash hit *Shakti*. The reuniting of Sippy, Bachchan and the super *Sholay* scriptwriting duo of Salin and Javed created a massively successful film with Bachchan and Dilip Kumar as father and son on opposite sides of the law. Tejawaini Ganti highlights that Bachchan was referred to as a "one-man industry" during this period, but not all his films were hits. The 1981

Silsila (*Affair*) is noted as the third biggest flop of the 1980s by Subhash K Jha. The modern film, directed by Yash Chopra, had a host of bankable names alongside Bachchan, including Shashi Kapoor and Sanjeev Kumar. But the film was rejected by audiences.

In many ways it marked the start of Yash Chopra's unsuccessful 1980's period. On paper the film looked good with a strong cast, contemporary script and leading ladies Rekha and Amitabh's wife, Jaya. Even this cast should have drawn an interested crowd as rumours were rife that Bachchan and Rekha were having an illicit affair and that Jaya was simply a trophy wife. In the film, Bachchan broods under the weight of his conservatism, a plotline that would reoccur in his successful return to screen in the noughties with *Mohabbatien* (2001) and *Kabhi Khushi Kabhi Gham* (2001).

Chopra also tried to invest in the idea of repeat value in the film, based on how many times the same person came to watch it. *Sholay* is the king of repeat value and in the late 1970s and early 1980s directors spent a considerable amount of time and energy trying to unlock repeat audiences. One method was to use unique foreign locations. In *Silsila*, Chropra included two love songs shot in tulip fields in Holland. Ganti suggests that the directors were trying to create "virtual tourism"(Ganti, 2004, p. 87) in their films. As most of the population were immobile, especially in relation to foreign travel, the idea often did prove a draw. Ganti again suggests that "despite the significant amount of money involved in foreign shoots, for both aesthetic and economic reasons, Hindi film-makers continue to find foreign location shooting an attractive option" (Ganti, 2004, p. 88). Regardless, the audience didn't find the tulips in *Silsila* attractive at all.

In 1983 the first of three life-changing events befell Bachchan.

While filming the Mahonnam Desai film *Coolie* (1983), he suffered a near life-threatening accident from a fall on set. He was admitted to hospital and an around the clock vigil quickly formed, not just outside the hospital, but next to televisions and radios across the country. The nation prayed for his recovery. It is said that the Prime Minister Indira Gandhi even cut short a state visit to the US to see her friend in hospital.

Amithabh the politician

The Big A, as Amithabh had become known, was to contended with far bigger trials in the 1980s. On 31 October 1984 Indira Gandhi was assassinated by her Sikh bodyguards at her official residence. In the months leading up to her death she had ordered army intervention in an internal battle for a Sikh homeland. The religious factions in India at the time were at loggerheads and the Sikh rebel leader Jarnail Singh Bindranwale was causing the government a significant problem with his secessionist struggle.

When Mrs Gandhi ordered an attack on the Golden Temple, the most significant Sikh shrine in India, she offended many of the Sikh faith. In the attack, Bindranwale was killed, but when her bodyguards assassinated her they felt they were avenging not him but their faith.

In the wake of her death violence erupted throughout India, but Delhi was particularly badly hit with more than 2,700 citizens killed in riots in the city, mostly Sikhs. In truly nepotistic fashion, her son Rajiv was elected Head of the Congress and Prime Minister. Rajiv and Bachchan were good friends and the star decided that he should support his friend and enter politics, so he stood as a member of parliament in his home city of Allahabad and won with a convincing majority.

But "this marked the beginning of the trial by fire which lasted about 15 years, leading to the almost total erosion of the legend that was Amitabh Bachchan" (Dasgupta, 2006, p. 94).

Bachchan entered politics with the approach he applied to the film industry. He was a crusader. In Allahabad, he paid for three mobile health trucks to deliver health care to the poorest areas of the city; he campaigned for financial transparency by public officials; he was an advocate of Rajiv's open economic policies and he championed the idea of greater freedom of information for the general public.

But politics is not the same as the film industry and many congress members disliked his approach, which they perceived as brash. This left Bachchan out in the cold four years later when he was involved in a political corruption scandal. The Bofor's arms deal effectively brought down Rajiv's government in 1989. The scandal, which surrounded the supply of Bofor's 155mm field howitzer to the Indian army, led to accusations of large kickbacks being received by members of the congress for the completion of the deal. Bachchan was named as one of the politicians who exerted his influence to pass the procurement bill in return for a financial incentive.

The scale of the corruption was unprecedented and he was destroyed politically. After the Swedish press broke the story the Indian Central Bureau of Investigations began an in-depth investigation. Bachchan was named among the suspects, as was the Prime Minister Rajiv Gandhi. The investigations led to the end of both men's political careers. Bachchan had made enemies in the congress and quickly found himself ostracised from the party. Without allies and mounting public opinion against him he resigned while still pleading his innocence. Rajiv continued to the general election, which his party lost badly in 1989. In the wake of the political shift away from the congress, Rajiv had his security detail reduced and he was assassinated in 1991 in a suicide bombing by a Tamil Tiger terrorist.

Bachchan's political and film careers were in tatters following his resignation from the congress. In Allahabad, his home town and constituency, residents burned effigies of him in disgust. Susmita Dasgupta summed up the national feeling towards him when she wrote:

> In a strange paradox, a whole nation that prayed for Amitabh's recovery in 1982 was by 1987 only too eager to believe that he had made money on the sly in the Bofor's deal. In a matter of five years, social economic and political conditions had changed dramatically and Amitabh Bachchan became the foremost and most well-known of the change. (Dasgupta, 2006, p. 70)

Life after politics: the fall and rise of a superstar

India had moved on from Bachchan's Vijay and Anthony stock characterisations of the super hits of the 1970s and early 1980s. The biggest problem was that the socially rebellious characters that he chose to play didn't seem to suit him anymore and audiences found it hard to suspend their disbelief when they watched him trying to fight against corruption on the screen.

In her book on Bachchan Susmita Dasgupta refers to him being "homeless"(Dasgupta, 2006, p. 102), a man without his industry. The 1988 film *Shahenshah* was typical of the films he made in his first comeback period. He plays a seemingly corrupt cop, who is actually a good man fighting for good and justice against the people's scourge and corruption. The problem here of course is one of life imitating art and art imitating life. It goes without saying that even the most avid Bachchan fan was displeased by this feeble attempt to speak to the public. The hugely unsuccessful *Ganga Jamuna Saraswati* (1988), *Toofan* (1989) and *Jaadugar* (1989) followed.

There were, however, two memorable films between his resignation and 1992. In 1990, he starred in the critically-acclaimed film *Agneepath* (*Path of Fire*), directed by Mukul Anand, where he returns to the character of Vijay. In essence, the film is a remake of *Deewar*, with some touches of Kapoor's *Awara* and displays the maturity of this new Vijay in comparison to the 1970's character of Deewar. The film also earned Bachchan a National Film Award for Best Actor. However *Agneepath* was not very successful at the box-office. Dasgupta believes that the film failed essentially because audiences had moved on; they were no longer interested in the contemplating, reflective leading man and Bachchan was becoming irrelevant in the emerging Bollywood of the 1990s. In 1991, he made a brief return to the top of the box-office throne with Mukul Anand's *Hum* (*Us*). But this success was short-lived and in the end he conceded that his career couldn't sustain the poor reception of the films of this period. In 1992 he called time on his acting career once more.

But unlike his departure into politics in the 1980s, Bachchan was not planning to leave the entertainment industry. His retirement coincided with the launch of the Amitabh Bachchan Corporation Limited (ABCL), which was set up with the intention of managing the Bachchan brand and also fostering new talent in the industry.

The industry was now awash with black money or money from illegal sources and ABCL sought to broker legitimate funds for producers and directors. The final element of ABCL was the management division. Bachchan wanted to bring a new air of professionalism to Bollywood, along the successful Hollywood lines. The idea was the creation of a management division that would manage the careers of Bollywood's stars, negotiate their contracts, deal with the ever hungry press and keep the vultures away.

Unfortunately for Bachchan, ABCL was the biggest and most costly flop of his career. It is true to say that the Indian entertainment industry in the pre-global market of the 1990s was not ready for the boutique style of services that it offered. The market was (and is, judging by Shah Rukh Khan's similar failure in this area) just too traditional and from a financial point of view the black market forces are still very strong. The failure of ABCL was one of the biggest collapses in Indian corporate history and triggered the personal bankruptcy of Bachchan.

The operational reasons for the failure of ABCL have been bounced around the Indian entertainment industry ever since. The sceptics always believed the corporation to have been set up as a cash cow for Bachchan and so were unsympathetic to the losses. The management claimed that he siphoned off the company's funds for his own gain, while he ascertains that ABCL's management mislead him as to the financial health of the company. Either way, Bachchan seemed to have finally played his last hand in Bollywood.

How was Bachchan now going to regain financial security, especially when you consider that it had taken him almost thirty years to gather the fortune that was subsumed into the failure of ABCL? The first step in rebuilding his career and his fortunes came from a television executive, Samir Nair, who offered Bachchan the opportunity to host a new TV quiz show called *Kaun Banega Crorepati*, which literally translates into *Who Wants to be a Millionaire?*

The Bachchan family and his advisors were cautious of this offer because of the poor development of television as an industry in India. By this time things were changing and the satellite television broadcasts of Star TV were revolutionising Indian entertainment habits. In short, the Bachchan family were being snobbish, feeling that the step down to the small screen would be the final comedown for the once great cinema star. But the outcome was the complete opposite. *Kaun Banega Crorepati* turned out to be the vehicle that single-handedly remodelled, relaunched and reinvigorated Bachchan's career.

One of the accusations against Bachchan during his career was that he was distant and remote, sitting God-like above his fans. When his world began to collapse after the Balfor Affair a fairly large amount of the industry and the press, who had disliked him, delighted in his ruin. The trick that *Kaun Banega Crorepati* allowed was that it beamed him into everyone's house not as a Vijay or a Jay or an Anthony. The man the audience reacquainted themselves with wasn't a character fighting against the social injustices of life in the developing modernity of independent India, but Bachchan himself. This allowed old fans to reconnect with their old hero, new audiences to delve into his back catalogue, and finally it allowed them to forgive him and forget the past.

The success of the quiz show propelled him back into the world of Bollywood. But he was no longer a social fighter. He had found a new character type, which was honest and true to his journey. In the 2000 film *Mohabbatein* (*Loves*) Bachchan unveiled his patriarchal father figure. A vision of modern India, he reflected the modern head of an Indian family dealing with the new age of globalisation and wealth and its effects on the fabric of Indian society. In *Mohabbatein* and in the 2001 film *Kabhie Khushi Kabhi Gham* (*Sometimes there's Happiness,*

Sometimes there's Sorrow) he performed as the strict patriarch who wants to govern his family along traditional lines, but in each film he relents and allows himself to change and morph into the modern Indian he must be to allow his family to survive.

Interestingly, these two massive comeback films saw him acting alongside Bollywood's new mega star, Shah Rukh Khan. Other notable films early in the millennium were the contemplative *Aks* (*Reflection*) in 2001 and the critically-acclaimed and internationally-renowned true story in the 2005 *Black*. Between these two films he also starred as the narrator in *Lagaan*. The success of these films and his return to the top table of Bollywood does however lie in his ability to reconnect with the audience, something he simply failed to do in the 1990s. The root of this success was his honesty; he was finally being true to himself and his audience for the first time since *Coolie* in 1983. This has been recently confirmed in his role as an ageing Shakespearian actor playing Lear in the English language film *The Last Lear* (2007).

Mani Ratnam's *Bombay*

Following the highs and lows of Bachchan's career, I will now focus on the work of Mani Ratnam, principally *Bombay* and *Dil Sè*. The latter starred the enigmatic Shah Rukh Khan (SRK) the current mega star of Bollywood. As he is so important the subsequent chapter then continues to discuss the life and films of SRK.

The 1990s saw a total shift in the Bollywood model. Bachchan's star was on the wane, the Gandhi political era was over, and India was entering a new chapter in its short history of independence. The over-riding message emerging from India's political and social voices was a revulsion of corruption, the black economy and anything else that held the Indian people back from making progress. This renewed vigour was the catalyst for an economic explosion that has created the emerging middle-classes and the wealth that has fostered the TATA empire and international sports philanthropy through a Formula One team (Force India) and English football club ownership (Queens Park Rangers and Blackburn Rovers). But this surge has also seen a rise in Hindu conservatism and a deepening rift in the relationship between India and its closest neighbour, Pakistan.

The social changes that engendered the Hindu conservatism and gripped Bombay in the early 1990s led to an escalation in the violence between Hindu conservative militia and the Muslim population. It quickly developed into full-scale riots and in a short space of time more than 2,000 people of both communities had died. Ratnam's film, *Bombay*, is set against these turbulent times in the newly-renamed city of Mumbai. Ratnam describes the film as a love story set against the inter-religious riots of 1992 and *Bombay* is a love story, but one of forbidden love between a Hindu man and a Muslim woman. The choice of the cross-community love story was a constructionist device to create the duo's moment of unity at the end of the film. But the choice of main characters could also be located in Ratnam's roots. Being a Tamil director from Madras places him in an interesting position, especially as the 1990s saw a continual escalation of the violence between the Tamil Tigers and the Indian government.

The Hindu right wing nationalist Shiv Sena party was in the ascendancy in Bombay in the 1990s. It secured control of the local government and in 1995, just before the release of the film, successfully changed the city's name back to it ancestral title of Mumbai. However, Ratnam has always insisted that regardless of the name change the film never had "alternative titles. It was always Bombay" (Gopalan, 2005, p. 16).

The Shiv Sena was uncompromising in its nationalism. It viewed the city as Hindu rather than a secular city that could accommodate all. The violence that sparked the famous riots of 1992 began as a result of a Hindu gang's destruction of the historic Muslim site of Babri Masjid on 6th December. The calculated attack led to reprisals on both sides and then pitched battles. This violence and fundamentalism ignited emotions on both sides, which lead to the riots of Bombay.

In the film, Ratnam creates a simple story of forbidden love. The romance is sparked early on when Shekhar sees Shaila Banu stepping from a ferry at a jetty, her veil blowing up by the wind to reveal the beauty of her face. The soft focus cuts of the scene are a beautiful representation of both the distances between their religions and their places in society. The fundamental representation of the distance between them is the fact that she wears a veil.

Shaila is seen for the first time in Bombay

Ratnam could easily have made Shaila a modern Muslim woman in India, like Farah Khan, the film's chorographer, but his decision to make her a traditional Indian Muslim woman allowed him the freedom to create two complementary plotlines, the first being the conflict between their families and the difficulty in a cross-cultural relationship in semi-rural India, and later mirroring this conflict in the religious turbulence of the Bombay riots.

The family conflict in the first half of the film is appeased in the second somewhat by the birth of the couple's two children in Bombay. Their arrival marks a pivotal moment, as it is their disappearance that draws the family into the madness and mayhem of the riots. Ratnam uses the children as an important emotive tool, the separation of the children from their parents creating the opening for the family to be drawn into the turmoil.

The juxtaposition of the family and the riots also has much wider overtones for Ratnam. As a liberal observer and as a Tamil from the south of the country, he is a keen desenting voice in Indian life and voices his dissatisfaction through his films. In *Bombay* he rallies against the Hindu fundamentalism threatening the secular Hindu and Muslim populations, who live in peace. In his 1997 film, *Dil Sè*, he directly attacks the progress of the country since independence in 1947. The fact that the film was released fifty years after independence is a measure of his calculated protest at the politics of the day.

Bombay had a troubled path to the cinema screen. Ratnam had to play a difficult game with the Bombay authorities and the national censors alike. Unfortunately, he also had to contend with the spectre of 'Black Money'. In India, the underworld's financial affairs are referred to as Black Money transactions and the Bollywood circus was a prime area for exploitation. Ratnam made a visible and concerted effort to avoid any association with Black Money, which usually brought with it certain demands such as the use of a certain actor in a role or the cutting of a film in a particular way.

Ratnam created independent production companies for his films, working at times with other notable film-makers like Shekhar Kapur. In 1993, he established Aalyam Productions, firstly to make *Thiruda Thiruda!* (*Thief! Thief!*) and then *Bombay* (it is worth noting that sometimes the title for this film is given as *Bumbai*, although the agreed title is *Bombay*) in 1994. He has always chosen to produce and self-finance his own films. It was during the troubled post-production stages that ABCL got involved in the distribution and the post-production financing of the film. Working with Bachchan's ABCL was a positive for Ratnam. Bachchan was always noted for his stance against the Black Money producers and distributors and he was also a Nehruist who believed in the socialisation project of Nehru's India, progressive and harmonious. He loved Bombay and would have been acutely aware of the politics of the Shiv Sena. His corporation's involvement was motivated politically just as much as it was motivated financially.

The mortally wounded ABCL was right to bank on the profitability of *Bombay*, and its hype. The film was contentious from the beginning. Both Hindu and Muslim communities opposed the religious representations in the film. The process of actually distributing it was difficult and involved local and national censors as well as profiteering cinema-owners who sought to capitalise on the demand for tickets. The censorship of the film was complicated by the reluctance of any regional authority to take responsibility for the ruling on the final certification or the related cuts that might be necessary.

Gopalan tracked the censorship route and is confident that the first submission to the Board of Censors was on 25 December 1994 in Madras. The regional officer in charge "reassured Ratnam that the film would receive a U certificate" (Gopalan, 2005, p. 24). But this was a new post holder in the Madras office and he was probably unaware of the political turmoil that was surrounding this film. The following day he informed Ratnam that he couldn't offer it a U certificate and that three major cuts would need to be made. Ratnam refused and in so doing sparked a chain of events that continued until March 1995. Normally, the Madras office of the Board of Censors would convene for a special hearing where Ratnam could plead his case against the cuts, but instead they sent the film to Bombay, perhaps because the film was definitely going to be released in Hindi as well as the Tamil version seen in Madras, or perhaps because of pending elections with the Shiv Sena. Such a controversial film might have sparked off fresh hostilities (even though the Bombay Police Department viewed and supported the film).

It is not surprising, then, that the Bombay office made the decision to send the print to the Home Department in the state, Maharashtra, which abstained from any responsibility for the certification of the film and passed the print on to the nation's capital and the Home Ministry in Delhi.

In the end, the Board of Censors enforced a total of seventeen cuts, broken down into seven sound, nine filmed sequences and a piece of news footage. One of the cuts stated that the violence in the film had to be reduced by 25 per cent. The depiction of innocent bystanders being killed in the crossfire was also to be removed and the police were to be spared. Images of the police firing on a crowd were to be deleted, as were the scenes of the lynching of a policeman and the brutal death of another. The cuts were obviously political and designed to reduce impact. There were dialogue cuts that may have been contentious, for example Afghanistan was not to be mentioned. But one of the most puzzling cuts was BBC News footage of the Babri Masjid being pulled down, footage which was already widely in use.

Ratnam was also confronted by the fact that the narrative of a Hindu-Muslim relationship was potentially dangerous. It is clear from the cuts and the tone of the authorities that the Hindu right wing had a considerable amount of momentum behind it and caused the board to fear a possible repeat of the violence.

It seems trivial to us in the West that a film could raise such concern. *Jerry Springer The Opera* (2003) and *The Passion of the Christ* (2004) caused some protests, but no-one was hurt. When the Hollywood actor Richard Gere kissed Shilpa Shetty during a presentation for his AIDs foundation, *The Times of India* reported that:

> In Varanasi, Shiv Sena and Bande Mataram Sangharsh Samiti activists as well as Muslims staged protests in various parts of the city and burnt effigies of Gere and Shetty to protest against their 'indecent behaviour' which, the protesters claimed, was 'an attack on our cultural

ethos'. In Kanpur, protesters, mostly students, burnt effigies and demanded that Gere should leave the country, while demonstrators in Bhopal threatened to boycott Shetty's forthcoming films. (*Times of India,* April 16 2007)

The reception of *Bombay* was just as dramatic as the storyline. The release was so contentious that the police departments of several cities, including Bombay, had to deploy sniffer dogs to check for bombs at cinemas before screenings of the film. Sporadic riots broke out in several cities and towns. Hyderabad was a particular flashpoint with hoax bomb threats, police inspecting theatres and the intimidation of cinema-owners. The majority Muslim population of the city led the protests, some of which turned to violence and looting. Under mounting pressure, the police commissioner took the difficult step of banning the film for a period of four months in the city. Lalitha Gopalan sheds further light on a particular incident in India's thirteenth largest urban conurbation, the town of Nagpur in the Maharashtra state. The film was released state-wide on 6 April 1995 and riots immediately erupted in Nagpur. Gopalan reports that during the first screening of the day

> … after intermission, fifteen to sixteen youths got up from their seats and shouted slogans demanding the banning of the film. They wanted a rampage, breaking chairs and huge glasses fitted to the foyer doors. As they stormed out of the theatre, about the same number of persons standing outside joined them in burning a poster of the film in the cinema. (Gopalan, 2005, p. 29)

On 14 of April 1995, the film was finally released in Bombay. The-then police commissioner Satish Sawhney had bowed to continued pressure from the Muslim community, which strongly felt that the film was anti-Islamic. Fearing violence, he had postponed the release to allow the Muslim protests to be heard by the authorities. So, twelve days after its initial release date, the film finally opened in the city. Tensions were high; the theatre was searched for bombs and suspect cars were towed away by police. It was important that the screening went smoothly. The Muslim community had issued a decree that Muslims should boycott the film but in the end the release was anti-climatic and the Muslim boycott, while supported by protests, didn't spark massive violence. Ratnam has consistently been accused of caving in to the Hindu right in Bombay to secure the release of the film. It is hard to know how true this is, but it is known the ABCL and Bachchan himself courted the Shiv Sena for approval. Gopalan reports that even Bachchan received death threats.

The Indian cinema website Upperstall.com doesn't mince its words in relation to the pro-Hindu sentiment:

> *Bombay*, a love story between a Hindu boy and a Muslim girl against the backdrop of the Bombay riots of 1993, ran into controversy as the film was released in Bombay only after getting clearance from Shiv Sena Chief Bal Thackeray. The film was attacked for its anti-Muslim stand, its misrepresentation of widely reported events in order to blame the Muslims for having started the riots and for its tendency to equate the 'voice of reason' with Hindu majority. But all the controversy helped the film as it scored heavily at the box-office. (Mani Ratnam | Upperstall.Com, n.d., p. 12)

Ratnam's controversial approach to film-making continued in the 1990s. The film *Dil Sè* (*From the Heart*) in 1998 is another example of his feelings about how far India has come since independence. But the film is actually far more famous for reasons other than the political standpoints of it director.

Firstly, it was a domestic flop, yet it was also a massive international success. It has one of the most memorable and often played dance sequences in Bollywood history. It launched the global careers of Farah Khan and AR Rehman, and it was a consummate vehicle for the self-declared king of Bollywood, Shah Rukh Khan.

SRK showing his moves in Dil Sè

Dil Sè is not a particularly good Bollywood film in a traditional sense, chiefly due to its convoluted narrative. The premise is fairly straightforward. An All India radio journalist is travelling to a disputed region of the country. While waiting to board a train he notices a beautiful stranger on the platform. In a strange twist of fate she turns out to be a terrorist and a member of the gang with whom he is trying to secure an interview. So far, so good. But their lives are too separate. He returns to Delhi to marry and she to her unresolved and desolate life. It is at this point that the film becomes more like a European film and less Bollywood-like. There isn't the sense of a happy resolution and even more perplexing are the strange narrative conventions.

Shah Rukh Khan may be Bollywood's most well-known actor, but I wouldn't be alone in citing that he is not the best actor in

Bollywood. He has a style (which we will discuss in more detail later) that needs careful management as well as direction. The odd radio broadcast scenes in the film are an indication of Ratnam allowing Khan to go over the top and they jar against the ordinary Bollywood style and turn Indian audiences off . According to Box Office India.com, in India the film made a net gross of 9,25,00,000 IRs, which is small change in relation to the 65,00,00,000 IRs made by the 1994 smash hit *Hum Aapke Hain Kaun* or the 66,44,00,000 IRs made by Shah Rukh Khan's 2001 smash hit *Kabhi Khushi Kabhie Gham*. Nevertheless, it was an international success, totalling of 8,30,00,000 IRs worldwide, with 3,30,00,000 IRs of that in the UK. This places the film 75th in the all-time overseas earners for Bollywood. Again it is a long way behind *Kabhi Khushi Kabhie Gham*'s second place with 36,75,00,000 IRs or *Hum Aapke Hain Kaun*'s 28th place and 15,50,00,000 IRs. But the film is at least credited with establishing Shah Rukh Khan internationally.

Shah Rukh Khan: Mr Bollywood

SKR enjoys a Starbucks in New York in Kabhi Alvida Naa Kehna

If you are a foreign multinational trying to inspire new customers to your exclusive brands you will choose the everyman of an industry as your spokesman. Tag Heuer, the watch company, recently enlisted the services of Lewis Hamilton, a Formula One champion. Why him? He is an ordinary boy from Stevenage in the UK, who made it. Pepsi has recently used European footballers in its campaign, including David Beckham. Why him? He was an ordinary boy from Essex who made it first at Manchester United and then across the world. Tag Heuer, unsurprisingly then, sought out Shah Rukh Khan to be the talisman for the company in India. Why? Tag Heuer says:

> With millions of fans and a series of films that are a testimony to his immense talent, SRK, as he is known, is king of the Indian film industry. Fifteen cinema awards, a successful production company, a perfume carrying his name and, above all, the adoration of a public who know what they like... the recognition Shah Rukh Khan enjoys today is the result of an unceasing search for excellence and tireless creativity. (Stars & Glamour, TAG Heuer Ambassadors, Shah Rukh Khan, Biography, n.d.)

Khan joined the likes of Uma Thurman, Tiger Woods, Jeff Gordon, Maria Sharapova, Lewis Hamilton, Heikki Kovalainen, Kimi Raikkonen, the late Steve McQueen, Peter Ho, Priyanka Chopra and Sebastien Bourdais in Tag Heuer's campaigns and lives amongst the glitterati of the global entertainment industry. But his rise to stardom was less meteoric than it might initially appear.

In many ways, his success runs parallel to the economic success of India in the post-Gandhi 1990s. As Bachchan's star began to set others had to replace him. SRK (as he is famously abbreviated) is just one of a successful group of young actors who broke through in the 1990s. Their emergence is inextricably linked to the rise in indigenous television and the digital and satellite revolution in Indian entertainment during the 1980s and early 1990s.

Born on 2 November 1965 in New Delhi, Khan was the second child of Meer and Fatima Khan. The family was not wealthy. Meer was educated, with a degree in law, but he was unlucky in business and the family was always one step away from financial ruin as his ventures collapsed. However, Fatima was dedicated to providing a stable and sheltered life for Khan and his sister, Shanaz. They were allowed to experience music and other cultural treats even thought the family finances couldn't support it. This was an important part of their childhood and it was this connection to the arts that undoubtedly has allowed Khan to thrive in a cut-throat business.

The Khans were Muslim, but both parents had very different views on how to raise their children. In Indian society, the separation of the classes and religions has always been an issue of contention. The India of the 1960s and 1970s in which Khan grew up were no different. The partition in 1947 still hung over the populations of India and Pakistan and the disputed region of Kashmir provided a flashpoint for the two armies. The nuclear proliferation of both countries also escalated tensions. Religion was never far from the agendas of the people; in many ways it defined them. Meer was a confirmed secularist. He was not a strict Muslim, nor did he bring up his children to be. In her book *King of Bollywood*, Anupama Chopra says how Meer was "devoutly secular and encouraged the same in his family... Unlike Fatima, Meer rarely fasted during the month of Ramadan" (Chopra, 2007, p. 30). Fatima was more connected to her religion, yet not strictly. Chopra tells us how "she endeavoured to say her namaaz (prayers) the prescribed five times a day" (ibid.). The divisions in the family's relationship with regard to religion was not a divergent issue for the growing Khan; it is again another example of how the building blocks of his everyman personality were derived from the structures of his upbringing.

On 19 November 1980, Meer died from cancer. Fatima was now left in financial peril with two children to support on her own. She was working at this time as a magistrate, but was forced into taking over the family's business interests - a restaurant and an oil brokerage. While Fatima had never shown any aptitude for business, she had an uncanny knack for it, far more so than her late husband, and the family restaurant prospered under Fatima until her death in 1991. Her decline into ill health was just as rapid as Meer's and troubled Khan greatly. He fell into a deep depression following her death and fled to start a new life in Bombay.

SRK attended St Columba's High School in Delhi. It was at this Christian Brother-run school that the secular Muslim boy began to be bitten by the drama bug. He was a founding member of the ultra cool C-Gang. Khan and his friends were much Westernised than many other students and sought out coveted Western material, from clothes to pop culture.

In 1983, the popular student (he graduated with the school's Sword of Honour in 1985) was cast in a production of *The Wiz*, a musical version of *The Wizard of Oz*. This was to be his first performance.

The experience of the school show was undoubtedly a factor in his career choice, but it was coupled with his almost unquenchable appetite for films. He was an avid film-goer and also put the family's video player to excellent use. However, it was theatre that initially hooked the young school graduate. In 1985, Khan was a member of Theatre Action Group, also known as TAG, which was set up by English expat Barry John in 1973 and ran until 1999. The TAG group was very well-respected in Delhi, even if stage drama was not the most popular or profitable of art forms. Khan was considered very lucky to have been taken on by and tutored by John, as it certainly gave him a grounding in the profession long before he made his big break.

The company was not professional in a financial sense; it resembled the fringe companies of today where the actors and artistic directors also hold down careers. The young Khan was a student at Hans Raj College, part of the University of Delhi. In the five or so years that he spent with TAG learning his craft he never really became the star of the group. He was a developing actor but was seen as too energetic, too much of a livewire to be able to sustain the more serious roles. He did, however, find a niche with the children's and school performances.

His first film, the New Wave flop *In Which Annie Gives it Those Ones* (1988) was as much odd as it was a poor choice. The film was always going to be at odds with his true ambition. The successful time he spent at TAG had instilled the awareness of the craft of acting in Khan, but he was not then, or now, a conventionally straight actor. He was passed over for the main part and instead given what was basically a featured extra role, a gay character – not the normal choice for an aspiring Bollywood star. But Khan completed the film and, if nothing else, he learnt from it that art house cinema was not for him.

His big break followed shortly after, although not in film as he had expected. Khan became a household name on television. India was almost thirty years behind the US in developing television as a major commercial force. The geographical size of the country, the collection of languages and dialects and the huge economic burden of distributing a TV signal to a population that the majority of could never afford a TV all conspired to delay the arrival of a decent service. *Fauji* was one of the new landmark mini-series created for Indian TV. But this was not SRK's first TV role. He was already working on Lakh Tandon's mini-series *Dil Dariya* (*River of the Heart*) as a Sikh boy. *Fauji*'s creator, the retired Colonel Raj Kapoor (no relation to the Kapoor dynasty) was a close friend of Tandon's and as a result managed to get Khan on set. The thirteen-part TV series followed a group of army recruits through their training to become commandos. Kapoor saw the series as his way of honoring the army and the series is not dissimilar to many coming of age stories. It was a runaway success and launched Khan into the limelight. But while popular, it was not the catalyst to the big time that he expected. The show was first aired in January 1989, but he still had to wait until 26 June 1992 for his first film to be released. Between *Fauji* and *Deewana* there were three other mini-series, the most notable being *Circus* and an adaptation of *The Idiot*, which earned him good reviews. The constant TV work got him noticed and he became a debutant of Bollywood alongside Aamir Khan just as the sun was setting on Bachchan's second film career. There was now a throne to fill.

With *Fanju* and *Circus*, Khan caught the eye of producers and agents, especially Viveck Vaswani. There was at this time stiff competition from other potential stars for Bachchan's crown. Salman Khan, Aamir Khan and, later on, Hrithik Roshan all looked the part. They represented the beautiful people, toned and immaculate, unlike Khan who had had an authenticity to him that maybe they didn't. There is also no doubt that there were differences in acting ability, but this is one of the key components of SRK - it's not just about the acting, for the fans actually buy into him, not the role.

It was this style of performance that might account for the period of time it took for him to really break through. Vaswani had put together a number of potential roles for Khan in 1991, but he was reluctant to make the move to Mumbai. It was the death of his mother that finally motivated him to leave Delhi behind and accept the roles available to him.

Raju Ban Gaya Gentleman (*Raju Becomes a Gentleman*, 1992), directed by Aziz Mirza and released in 1992, was a rags to riches story of a young and ambitious Mumbai engineer. The story was seen as a direct reference to Raj Kapoor's *Shree 420* and also referenced the corruption that had hampered national prosperity for so long. It is a moral tale reminding the audience not to compromise their traditions on the way to the top. In his 1992 film *Deewanna* (*Crazed Love*, 1992), Raj Kanwar broke with tradition somewhat by having the heroine as a widow who remarries, but that was as non-formulaic as the plot strayed. The main character, Ravi, is presumed dead after his wife's father arranges for him to be beaten up. After some time his wife finds love again with Raja (Khan) and they marry, but only for Ravi to return one day, to find his wife remarried.

After these two films Khan made *Chamathker* (*Miracle*, 1992), directed by Rajiv Mehra. It is a romantic comedy/ghost story/

gangster film with Khan playing the gullible Sunder who is betrayed by the ghost of a dead gangster who wants to do some good. He followed it with the weighty Malini's *Dil Aashanana Hai* (*The Heart Knows the Truth*, 1992) and Rakesh Roshan's *King Uncle* (1993), a two-hero film in the *Sholay* tradition. Of all of these 1992 films only one appears in the top 50 earners for 1990-1999 on indiaboxoffice.com. *Deewana* is ranked 33rd with a net gross of 21,53,00,000 IRs, yet is only rated as an average success. The first year of Khan's film career was a busy one, yet his wife Gauri and he were still only eking out a living. Two films in 1993 would begin to change that.

In 1993, Shah Rukh released five more films, two of which would begin to get him noticed in a very positive way. The first of these was *Baazigar* (*Gambler*, 1993), a film that every other leading man in Bollywood turned down on account of the lead being a violent, revenge-obsessed villain, totally devoid of any feeling or remorse. It was a risky move for the second year star, but a successful one. This film was not just memorable for Khan's nasty streak but it also showcased a new talent in Shilpa Shetty. We may only know her for her turn in *Celebrity Big Brother* but to date she has made 50 films and won a best newcomer award for the film.

The second successful film of 1993 was Yash Chopra's *Darr* (*Fear*, 1993), a dark, twisted love story and another script that many heart-throbs would have turned down. Khan's character is an obsessed stalker who terrifies Krian, a girl he first encounters at college. The film has some awkward moments; one disturbing scene occurs when SRK's character Rahul stages the suicide of an already dead man who everyone knew had a soft spot for Krian. By framing him, SRK's character buys himself some time, and he follows the couple to

Switzerland to kill Sunil and marry Krian. There is, of course, an unfortunate ending and Khan dies a villain's death at the hands of the wounded hero, Sunil. Bad or not, Khan became a star on the back of the success of these two films, with *Darr* being a particularly successful box-office hit, ranking as the 20th highest grossing film of the 1990s. The most interesting point about these two films was that Khan filmed them at the same time, flitting between sets, yet both villains remain different and precise to the films they appear in.

One of the biggest Indian films of all time was the 1995 *Dilwale Dulhania Le Jayenge* (*The Brave Hearted will take the Bride*). It was the second-highest grossing film of the 1990s with 98,33,00,000 IRs net adjusted gross earnings, which also places it fifth in the all-time earners' list from Bollywood. This mega blockbuster was to transform Khan from the promising superstar to a stratastar.

The film was based in London, European cities and the Punjab, the use of these locations capturing the new wave of internationalism in India. It was not the first film to use other locations - *Darr* was shot on location in Switzerland - but this film caught the rising *zeitgeist* that India was an emerging world power of industry and economics,. It also appealed to the rising difficulty of marrying traditional national values and Western ideals that were now impacting more and more in Indian life. Normally referred to as *DDLJ* for short, the film is a romance, but with a focus on the younger culture's disaffection with traditional norms. It does, however, resolve the need to respect the traditional as a way of maintaining the status quo of society.

The film is based around the brash exploits of Raj, the son of an Indian immigrant in London who has made it. Raj lives a lavish lifestyle with sports cars and endless money. He fails his university courses and yet is rewarded by his father for aspiring to be his own man. But all this is challenged when he meets Simran, the daughter of an immigrant who is a newsagent in London. The story revolves around the forbidden love between the non-traditional and Westernised Raj and the conservative and traditional Simran. Their love blossoms when they travel with friends during the summer on the Eurorail. Raj falls for her, but her conservative father has already arranged her wedding in the Punjab. She is unexpectedly taken from Raj's life to India to get married. Raj travels to the Punjab and immerses himself in the village to try and win her hand in a traditional way. The film captures the difficult decisions in a young Indian's life, particularly the issue of an arranged marriage.

Chopra describes the formulas for this film when she writes:

> Traditionally, Bollywood heroes make their debut with a DDLJ-style romance. The time-honoured formula is simple: boy meets girl, boy loses girl, boy gets girl, and they walk into the sunset hand in hand. The plot is designed to give the actor enough opportunities to show that he is worthy of being a star. He romances, dances, fights, and lip synchs melodious songs. Bollywood wisdom dictates that the love story is the safest way for a new face to win over viewers. (Chopra, 2007, pp. 135-136)

Interestingly, when you search for fan sites and blogs of *DDLJ* you tend to see a lot of people on their blogs referring to Raj as "a second-generation NRI". The idea of the NRI (non-resident Indian) is very important to the success of the film and the lucrative overseas market. Tejaswini Ganti says that "the film brought about a change in the representation of Indians settled in the West and led to the wealthy and the culturally authentic NRI character becoming a staple in contemporary

Hindi cinema" (Ganti, 2004, p. 170).

The most interesting thing about the successful NRI film is the international revenue. *DDLJ* was an unquestionable success at home. It played for five continuous years in theatres and broke *Sholay*'s long-standing mantle of longest-running film in India, but its real success lay elsewhere. In 1994, the excellent *Hum Aapke Hain Koun* (*Who am I to you*, 1994) was released and was a smash hit at home. But the real success of the film lay abroad with NRI audiences in the UK and the US. The film made a combined total of 15,50,00,000 IRs worldwide with 8,00,00,000 IRs in the UK alone. One year on and *DDLJ* was now primed to tap into this lucrative market. The astute choice of staging the film partly in London also made the film attractive to UK NRIs who could engage and associate with the more difficult situation of marrying traditionally in a Western country. *DDLJ* made a staggering 17,50,00,000 IRs one year later with 9,00,00,000 IRs in the UK.

The film propelled Khan into the international limelight, and also brought back an air of excitement around Bollywood in the UK. In fact, BoxofficeIndias.com's top ninety overseas earners' list only shows eight pre-2000 films with the oldest made in 1994 - SRK is in half of them. This is important in relation to *Dil Sè*. By all accounts, Ratnam's film was a domestic flop, but on the back of successful films like *DDLJ*, it was became successful overseas and is rated as the 78th highest overseas earner in Bollywood. In films like *Kuch Kuch Hota Hai* (*Something is Happening*, 1998), the 2001 *Kabhi Khushi Kabhi Gham* (*Happiness and Tears*, 2001), also known as *K3G*, and the 2003 *Kal Ho Naa Ho* (*Tomorrow May Never Come* Khan excels as the modern Indian man, the progressive NRI.

In 1999, SRK set up Dreamz Unlimited, a production company with Juhi Chawla and Aziz Mirza. Its first film was *Asoka* (2001), the historical epic about the famous Indian emperor Asoka. The film, while visually impressive, lacks gravitas, mainly because Khan bounces across the screen in the same exuberance of his *Dil Sè* days. It was a total flop. It only netted 7,25,00,000 IRs and doesn't even make it into the top fifty films of the noughties. It didn't even do particularly well overseas. But it marked the end of a run of blips for SRK and soon after he regained his box-office mojo. But while he was gallivanting with *Asoka*, something very exciting was happening with Bollywood, and most surprisingly he wasn't part of it.

Lagaan: Land Tax

Aamir Khan as Bhuvan steps up to bat against Captain Russell's men

This chapter on *Lagaan: Once upon a time in India* (2001) is very short and in a way to the point. This could be a discussion on Aamir Khan's success as one of Bollywood's biggest stars of all time, but I decided to let what is probably his greatest film do the talking for him. I have singled out this film for a technical reason, as it breaks with the normal generic production traditions of the national cinema, but over and above that, students love it. I was genuinely overwhelmed by the real connection students felt to this film and their ability to really appreciate it fully. For this reason alone it is worthy of a full chapter in this book.

Mother India was the last notable Indian film before *Lagaan* to do two things - secure an Oscar nomination and record using synchronised sound. Aamir Khan's wonderful *Lagaan* reinvented the Bollywood machine. The songs were in context, the romance was Western in that the boy might not get the girl after all, and the story was appealing not just to indigenous Indian audiences and NRIs but also to foreign language cinema-viewers worldwide. In 1998, *Dil Sè* flopped in India, yet was the first Hindi film to break into the British top 10 film's chart, and five years later *K3G* rose to number three in the chart. *Lagaan* made more then *Dil Sè*, but far less then *K3G*, yet it is a much better film than either of the previous two for it is a truly international text. The film should also be remembered as one of the only foreign language films to make a serious breakthrough with cricket at its very heart.

In his book *Balham to Bollywood*, Chris England, who plays the British soldier and cricketer in *Lagaan*, recounts how he first came to know Khan:

> I stuck the tape in and gave *Mela* a go. I recognised Aamir from the soft focus publicity shots on his fan club website. All I could say after watching a bit of Mela was that if he was the naturalistic one, then the rest of Bollywood must be populated with hams that would give messrs Sinden and Callow a run for their money. (England, 2002, p. 20)

The magic of *Lagaan* is that Khan really does give a naturalistic performance, albeit a Bollywood version of naturalism. But this objectively non-formulaic performance allowed the narrative to flow in more of a Hollywood fashion then previously seen in modern Bollywood films.

The story of *Lagaan* is simple. The local lords collect an agricultural tax each year based on the harvest and the British then take their share of this. The stereotypical imperialist Captain Russell decides to double the tax, knowing the villagers can't pay, meaning the lands can be confiscated. A young villager called Bhuvan challenges the tax and is made an offer by Russell: beat the English at cricket and pay no tax or lose and it will be trebled. Much to the scorn of the villagers Bhuvan accepts the challenge. There then begins a race against time to learn cricket and to beat the English. The story aside, the film looks good. It has a professional quality that is sometimes lacking in Bollywood films and the script and the direction also stand out.

But the really notable aspect of *Lagaan* is the use of synchronised sound. Since 1955, all Bollywood films have been made with noisy sets and lip synching. One of the key reasons for the success of the film was this move towards traditional Western film-making. *Lagaan* was not as successful as *K3G* but instead it actually earned something far more valuable. What *Lagaan* lost in revenue to *K3G*, it gained in the priceless currency of international kudos, with the American Academy and many other international audiences. *Lagaan*'s success was actually as a foreign language film, with the middle class foreign film audience not just the NRI's; it was a crossover film, something *K3G*'s substantially formulaic narrative couldn't ever achieve.

The Parallel Cinema

Satyajit Ray, India's most famous director

This chapter looks at India's parallel cinema and its most famous auteur, Satyajit Ray. This chapter also allows me the opportunity to discuss the censorial difficulties faced by parallel film-makers and the more positive reception these films are afforded in the West.

The world of Bollywood is a bubble in which the great and the beautiful live and act. They are the style icons of Indian history and the modern marketers, endorsing anything and everything that their adoring public will in turn seek to purchase. Bollywood is the glitz and glamour, it is safe and secure (even when edgy). In a country as vast as India there is room for only one main attraction. But there is an alternative to Bollywood, a film style much more in tune with the Western art house styles. Unlike Bollywood, this parallel cinema is genuinely edgy; it doesn't soften the blows of the story or the director with formulaic song and dance routines, and instead it exposes the whole narrative to the audience.

Satyajit Ray is considered to be the father of postcolonial art house Indian cinema. His controversial exposé of the conflicts apparent in the traditional and the modern ways of life in 1950s India sparked a censorial debate and purge that few expected. During the British period, censorship was administered by the Indian Cinematograph Committee. The state would hand over formal jurisdiction to the police and a board of censors who would then give a film a licence to be shown or would withdraw it if they felt it necessary. There was a general feeling in India at this time that strong censorship was necessary. Gandhi's call to retreat from Western values struck a chord with many Indians who saw Western ideals as a threat to the traditional way of life. The irony is that Ray's *Pather Panchali* (1955) raised these issues but became a text that changed the censors' views of Indian films, especially those screened abroad.

Ray was born into a gifted family of artists and writers, but his story is far from straightforward. He was born in West Bengal in 1921. His father, Sukumar, was a celebrated Bengali writer, photographer and painter, whose father was also a respected painter and writer. Sukumar inherited his father's Bengali children's magazine. But in 1924 he tragically died after a short illness. The family was plunged into poverty and Ray was sent to live with his cousins while his mother worked as a craft teacher.

In some ways his story is not dissimilar to Bachchan's. While Bachchan had the family connection to Nehru, Ray had a close family tie to the Bengali writer, poet and academic Rabindranath Tagore, considered to be one of the great minds of Indian literature. Tagore was championed in Europe by the Irish playwright and poet WB Yeats, who said of him: "I know of no man in my time who has done anything in the English language to equal these lyrics" (Foster, 1998, p. 469).

It was fortunate that this esteemed family friend became Ray's patron and principal muse. If the blessing of his artistic genetics was not enough, the patronage of the 1913 Nobel Prize winner for Literature certainly was. Tagore's influence on Ray was immense. In an interview with Folke Isaksson in 1970, Ray admitted that it was Tagore who wanted Ray to come and study at his college in Santiniketan, but that all the staff at the college contributed to his development; however, it is undeniable that Tagore's writings had a considerable effect on Ray and inspired him in his career.

Ray has made many films, but it is the *Apu Trilogy* and *Pather Panchali* in particular that have really captured the imagination of Western film aficionados. This odd Indian entry at Cannes in 1956 almost went unnoticed. This was the dawn of the new wave in Europe. The style had moved on from the brilliance of Italian Neo-realism and was giving way to the pop culture-fuelled jump cut style of the French New Wave directors. At Cannes the film was originally only scheduled for a morning screening, which would have consigned it to complete obscurity. Some members of the jury sought to redesignate its importance, and succeeded in moving the screening to come directly after Kurosawa's latest offering, *Ikimono no kiroku* (*I Live in Fear*, 1955), which was a Palme d'Or nominee.

The screening of *Pather Panchali* at this time was both a blessing and a curse. A sizeable chunk of the jury withdrew to a party thrown by the Japanese delegation, possibly to position Kurosawa into a Palme d'Or winning situation, but on the plus side French film critic André Bazin officially complained at the scandal of the judges withdrawing from the screening of *Pather Panchali* in such a way. His protests led to a rescreening. The jury were so mesmerised by the beauty and simplicity of the text that they voted it Best Human Document, a huge feat for a first-time Bengali director whose film could have been missed completely.

What makes *Pather Panchali* so very special is that it still remains relevant and attractive to both Western audiences and film academics alike today. It is simply a beautiful film. It has a patience and a stillness about it that transforms the mundane existence of its characters to a tangibly cathartic level for its audiences. There is an attention to detail that is so incredibly precise that each frame has the power to arrest the viewer in many ways. Ray talks of how when watching Godard the audience is actually drawn to the shaky edges of the frame as the hand-held *cinéma vérité* distorts the *mise- en-scène*. The construction of each shot in *Pather Panchali* is an attack on your senses, as the drama of Apu and his family unfolds in a simple and, at times, very matter of fact way.

Ray used predominantly untrained actors in the film, a decision that generates a sense of realism similar to the excellent performances of the real street children in Boyle's *Slumdog Millionaire*. His choice of style was heavily influenced by his relationship to Italian Neo-realist cinema, which came to prominence in early post-war Italy. The Italian film industry was arguably the biggest in Europe before the outbreak of the Second World War, but after the Allied victory the industry was in tatters. The Milanese studios were all but destroyed and the abject poverty of the Italian nation made the regeneration of the industry a distance dream.

Film-makers like De Sica therefore chose a different path. They decided to remove themselves from the confines of a studio and use the rubble-strewn cities as their studio instead. In the absence of trained, studio-contracted actors, they would use real people and their subject matter would be the simple lives of the Italian public. De Sica's *Bicycle Thieves* (1948) was a real inspiration to Ray who saw the film on his arrival in London. He said:

> In 1950 I went to England, just in time to see the early
> Neo-realist films. I suddenly realised that films like De
> Sica's *Bicycle Thieves* were made very cheaply, with non-
> professional actors. This really opened my eyes. On the
> boat back from England, I wrote the entire shooting script
> of *Pather Panchali*. (Cardullo, 2007, p. 8)

Ray struggled to finance the film and so resorted to self-
funding the project. It is even reported that he pawned his
wife's jewellery to do so. He also worked full-time at the
British-owned Calcutta advertising agency DJ Keymer while
shooting. Production began in 1952. Ray had approached all
the usual film producers in Bombay but there were a couple
of problems. First, the Indian pitch is very loose. The most
important issue is who has agreed to be in it and who is doing
the music and the songs. The story is generally no more than
a synopsis and a script is not important. Ray came to his
pitch meetings armed with detailed sketch books depicting
stage designs, shot plans and a fully-ready shooting script.
To his surprise, the producers simply wanted to know where
the songs were and were dismayed that there were none.
Needless to say, he struggled to secure any backers. In
mid-1952 he approached the West Bengal State Government
which, in a very unusual move, gave him 200,000 IRs to
complete the film. It was this government funding that sealed
the production security, and in 1956 prompted the central
government to establish a national film fund for the production
of non-Bollywood texts.

After independence, the censorship remained just as strict.
The new national Central Board of Film Censors coordinated
the different and diverse local Boards of Censors into a
coherent national group. It was this national group that
took exception to elements of Ray's work. The post-colonial
India was trying to redefine what it meant to be Indian in the

twentieth century; the new India would be an industrial nation to be proud of. The quasi-socialist montage of agricultural mechanisation at the beginning of *Mother India* is a clear example of this. The film highlights the modern India in the present tense of the text, and then depicts the hardship and poverty of the people in the past tense. Ray did not do this with *Pather Panchali*. His film was set very much in the present contemporaneous tense of 1950s post-colonial India. The difficulty for the audience is the lack of reconciliation of the two worlds. The life of Apu and his family and the modern landscape of electricity pylons and express trains are beautifully juxtaposed with the struggle of the endemic poverty of an independent India. In an interview in 1970, Ray said that these trains represented the journey between "rural and metropolitan India"(Cardullo, 2007, p. 43), but the censors were unhappy with this real and present depiction of Indian life and especially the depiction of the rural population as almost forgotten in time.

In *Pather Panchali*, Ray paints a world time has forgotten. Cloth covers the windows, not glass. Food is prepared in traditional ways with the woman of the house grinding her own wheat. The world highlights the fact that for many, independence didn't actually mean anything. In the rural areas life continued as it had done previously. Ray's presentation is one that may be unremarkably similar in some areas even today. In such a vast state it is completely possible that the Asian, and in particular the Indian, economic tigers will have gone unnoticed. It is possible that the credit crunch crisis of 2008 and the worldwide recession will also be unknown in the remote rural areas. The reason for this lies in the certainty that poverty is a fundamental part of Indian society. It was the fear that might be sparked off in the general public, especially the combustible urban populations, of the representation of

Apu and his sister Durga explore their world in Pather Panchali

this poverty, which forced the censors to make a ruling in the aftermath of the international success of *Pather Panchali*.

In 1952, Dr BV Keskar became the Minister for Information and Broadcasting. He was not so much a fan of censorship but a politician who in a very conservative way saw the merits of protecting the morals of the uneducated masses in Indian society. In the Bengali weekly news magazine *The Statesman* in 1956 he summed up his overall philosophy on why the Indian population needed protection from insidious texts:

> Films in Indian languages are meant for and seen by the mass of the people, most of whom are not educated... Now, the mass in any country is to some extent conventional, has certain prejudices that cannot be helped. An intellectual or educated audience can forgive or even appreciate unconventional themes or ideas put on the screen. The same cannot be said of the bulk of the people. I am afraid that this fact is conveniently forgotten.

Unfortunately, government cannot forget it because it is elected by the mass of the people and it has to take into consideration their feelings and sentiments. (In Barnouw, 1980, pp. 218-219)

It is interesting then that *Pather Panchali* caused such concern. The film, which was released in its original Bengali, did not transfer across the entire nation in the same way as, say, *Awara* could. Its language was alien to the majority of Indian inhabitants. Hindi as the national language allowed everyone to understand a text, and while the popular films were dubbed into myriad of different languages, *Pather Panchali* wasn't. There was little point in spending money that Ray didn't have in dubbing a text that might not yield the cost of the dubbing in ticket sales. There was also no point in using subtitles; literacy standards were so low that people simply couldn't read the words, regardless of their meaning. In essence, the film became an early Sunday matinee in the wider Indian theatrical release. So there was no need to protect the masses from it, or was Keskar actually afraid of the middle and upper class responses to *Pather Panchali*? He didn't want to start any sort of middle class revolt about the pace of development in the newly-independent India.

The film had been part-financed by the West Bengal Government, which was overjoyed at its success. The autonomy that followed elevated Ray to visionary status. But many in central government were torn by the film. They were pleased that an Indian film-maker had finally made it in the Western film industry. But they also felt that Ray had brought the country into disrepute. His highlighting of provincial poverty flew in the face of the projected images of India. These central officials felt that the film harmed the West's perception of India.

Ray was philosophical about the censors' opinion of the film and their worries in relation to the representations of rural Indian life. In an interview with Chidananda Das Gupta in 1962 he discussed the issues. Das Gupta pushed the accusation that Ray is guilty of only depicting the tragedies of Indian life. Ray felt that the overall feeling "is one of hope" (Cardullo, 2007, p. 10) and not tragedy. He continued by saying that "it isn't the business of the films to be constructive". This broadside at the safe Bollywood mainstream industry brings out his true influences, dominated by the Italian Neo-realists. When Das Gupta pushed him on the relationship with the central government, he would only admit that "they didn't want me to export *Pather Panchali*, they still don't" (Cardullo, 2007, p. 10). In many ways Ray's films exist because of the international recognition that *Pather Panchali* received at Cannes on its release. The immense international pressure and praise meant that the central government and the board of censors simply had to stand back from the Indian film-maker, who the West believed to be a national treasure.

The board of censors feared that the success of *Pather Panchali* might cause a rush of other Neo-realist inspired texts, which could harm India's preferred image in the West. As a result, the central government outlined a new approach to international distribution. In September 1956, the film magazine *FilmIndia* reported on the new position:

> The government of India has directed that before any State Government sends films – features or documentaries abroad for exhibition, the State Government should ascertain the film's suitability from the point of view of external publicity by the External Affairs [department]. (In Barnouw, 1980, p. 232)

The most important aspect of this censorship directive is the date - it quickly follows the 1956 release of *Pather Panchali*. The central government issued the changes as direct result of *Pather Panchali* and in particular the Bengali State Government's involvement in its production, and subsequent international distribution. Later, the Board of Censors extended the remit of its censorship listings of inflammatory situations to include "abject or disgusting poverty" (Barnouw, 1980, p. 14), a small line that remains an issue in Indian censorship laws today. One of the most unusual situations is that Danny Boyle and his *Slumdog Millionaire* production team have had the same issues and debates surround their film, but sixty years on.

Post-Satyajit Ray

Ray's success in bringing a successful naturalist approach to Indian cinema proved to be an inspiration to a different breed of Indian film-maker, whether it be Kaizad Gustard's socially challenging gay romp *Bombay Boys* (1998), Shekhar Kapur's disturbing and vivid *Bandit Queen* (1994), or Nair's beautifully crafted *Monsoon Wedding* (Nair, 2001). Each of these film-makers has the inspirational path clearing of Ray to thank for their ability to not just make the films that they wanted to, but also secure the audiences in both India and the West. The three texts draw on the Western model of film and not the formulaic Bollywood model. Yet music, and in two cases dance, are narrative elements in the films. Their real beauty is their ability to interweave music and song into the texts, yet avoid the clichés associated with them.

In 1994, the most unlikely of directors caused a stir which continued for two years in Indian cinema. Shekhar Kapur's Channel 4-funded *Bandit Queen*, based on the life of outlaw

Bandit Queen doesn't shy away from the instances of abuse in Devi's life story

turned politician Poolan Devi, was banned by the Board of Censors. Kapur's biggest hit had been with the second highest grossing film of 1987, the Bondesque comedy *Mr India*. Indeed, the jump from the slapstick of *Mr India* to the gang rape scenes of *Bandit Queen* is difficult to reconcile, but it is still successful.

Bandit Queen tells the chronological story of Poolan Devi, a poor, low caste woman who was sold as a child bride for a rusty bicycle and a goat by her father. As soon as the film begins it is obvious that this is not a Bollywood film. The young girls in the river discuss men and there is continual swearing, especially the repeated use of the word "sisterfucker". The vibrant colours, a hallmark of Kapur's work, frame the film in a suitable reality. But it is the sexual subject matter which actually charges it and makes it a censorial target.

From the time Devi is married, her life and sexual abuse become interlinked. The dominance of the Thuker men, the upper caste men, is continually reinforced through the use of sex as a weapon. In real life, Devi was abused at an early age and Kapur doesn't shy away from both the difficult issues of child brides and what is effectively sexual abuse and later the repeated raping of Devi and her desensitisation to life and normality as a result. When you consider the statement made by Dr Keskar in 1952, the Board of Censors had a considerable amount to consider with this film, not least the threat of social disturbance. There was a real fear that this film could have sparked riots as a result of the depiction of the police and the upper castes. The other difficulty for the censors was the issue not just of nudity but of sexual assault, rape and other violent crimes perpetrated against women.

On his official website Kapur says:

> My own favourite film of mine is *Bandit Queen*. It was born out of an anger I felt not only against what I saw, but also against myself because of not having seen it before. And I believe it caused people to pause and question by making them angry. Often the anger is expressed against the artist, but that's *ok*. (Shekharkapur.com, n.d.)

Mani Ratnam also faced the same anger directed at him in the wake of *Bombay*, which is a mainstream Bollywood film. Yet because *Bandit Queen* was outside the mainstream it already carried a stigma. It is hard to really pinpoint the Central Board of Film Censors' reasons for the banning of the film on its 1994 release. The charge of nudity was technically correct, but harsh. The depiction of women was unfavourable but factually based on the biography of Devi's life in the book *Bandit Queen*. The film was sexually explicit in many ways but again it was factual, albeit uncomfortably so. Were the censors directly opposed because of the perceived reception of the film, or were they pressurised by the heroine of the story? Devi was unhappy at the release of the film. As the script was based on the biography of her life she didn't have the copyright laws on her side. She did now have a new life as a member of parliament, and presented herself as the champion of the poor and oppressed. But she also had a book waiting to be published. Devi had written her autobiography entitled *I, Phoolan Devi*. The book, published by Warner Books, was set for a 1996 release and was being written as *Bandit Queen* was released. Unsurprisingly, Devi disowned the film, criticising it for lacking factual authenticity. *The Washington Post* alludes to this when in June 1995 Desson Howe's article 'India's Avenging Bandit' on the film stated:

> The real Devi initially took legal action to prevent the movies exhibition in India. She said she wanted to maintain her privacy. But she recently changed her tune and now stands behind the film. Still pending is whether director Kapur will make several specified cuts that the Indian censors have stipulated. (Howe, 1995, p. 42)

The debacle over the release of the film in India rumbled on, while internationally it was proving a hit. The backing of Channel 4 Films made it a credible indie film. The fact it was Indian and accessible also drew a crowd. In fact, when the film was finally released in India it picked up two Filmfare awards, one for direction and the coveted critics' choice. The release in India only occurred as a result of a High Court battle as Kapur tried to fend off the cuts imposed by the censors. In the end he had to agree to two specific cuts. Khalid Mohammed in *The Times of India* on 14 February 1996 quoted Kapur in relation to Devi and her opposition to the film's release. Kapur said:

> The film could be released in India only because she wanted it to. She had almost won the case in the Delhi court. The film had been banned. She agreed to its release

if she was given a certain amount of money and if two cuts – the love-making scene in Kanpur and the rape by Baba Gujjar – were carried out. The scenes were cut in accordance with the high court order at her request. (Mohammed, 1996).

Kapur also admitted that Channel 4 Films had paid her £40,000 for her cooperation. But the damage was done. The film was tarnished in the eyes of the population. Mohammed in the same article reports how the cinemas in Mumbai had to resort to "ladies only" screenings because of the reported behaviour of the male audience. The other sizeable problem for Kapur was the now non-existent relationship between the censors and the conservative Indian population who fanned the flames of negative feeling against the film, calling them "self appointed parallel censors". It might not be surprising then that in 1998 Kapur's stunning *Elizabeth* fell foul of the censors too.

Elizabeth should have marked a watershed in Indian cinema. Not just a commercial success but a hugely acclaimed film, it could only reflect well on the country of its director. *Elizabeth* won an Oscar for Best Make Up and was nominated for six more, including Best Picture and Best Actress. In all it won thirty international awards and was nominated for an additional thirty-two. But while the film was causing a sensation around the world the Central Board of Film Censors was unhappy. *The Times of India* reported that in August 1998 the censors demanded three cuts in *Elizabeth*, which were said to cause horror. The angered Kapur responded: "The Indian censors board makes an absolute mockery of the maturity of the Indian audience. It demeans the mindset of the very people who have the power and the intelligence to vote for their own government".

Monsoon Wedding *deals with contemporary Indian issues, but in a very western way*

Kapur's protests seemed very valid. Spielberg's *Saving Private Ryan* (1998) was released just before *Elizabeth*, but sailed past the censors. The intense horror of that film was deemed acceptable, but *Elizabeth* was not. The apparent inequalities in the Central Board of Film Censors is one of the reasons for Kapur's, and many others', frustrations.

Monsoon Wedding, traditional values and modern sentiment

Mira Nair's Golden Lion and Golden Globe winning *Monsoon Wedding* is a beautiful film filled with the colour and vibrancies of her beloved Delhi. The film is truly parallel in its construction. It maintains an authentic Hindi atmosphere but in a way that Western audiences can easily interact with. It is unusual in that it is just as accessible for a mainstream audience as *Bend it Like Beckham* (2002) or *East is East* (1999), yet it is a far superior film.

The narrative is a discourse on the place of tradition and family in modern India and the importance of NRIs in the development of the country. The depiction of NRIs in the cinema has become more popular as Bollywood steps out from its Mumbai confines and seeks to liven up narratives with better locations. In fact, the mainstream Bollywood producers are now actively seeking stories that can use NRIs. The simple economic reason for this is that if you make a film in New York about a group of non-resident Indians living successfully, you spread the positive national propaganda of the success of the country and you also get fantastic backdrops for your song and dance routines. This was the exact point of the highly successful and critically-acclaimed 2006 Karan Johar film *Kabhi Alvida Naa Kehna* (known in the USA as *Never Say Goodbye*) and was fundamental in the narrative of the 2001 Rahul Raichand smash hit *Kabhi Khushi Kabhie Gham*, which was partly set in England.

In *Monsoon Wedding* the narrative is based solely on the wedding of the fiercely independent and ultra-modern Aditi Verma to an NRI, Hemant, who is based in Texas. It is further complicated by the fact that Aditi is also having an affair with a TV producer. The struggle that she has between her emotions, her duty and her independence encapsulate the narrative but don't hide the powerful subplots. While the wedding has many stories that surround the stressed father Lalit and the rebellious mother Pimmi, they do not hide the two juxtaposed and socially challenging subplots. The first is a simple love story between the foppish wedding organiser PK Dubey and the lower caste maid. The love story is almost Coen Brothers-esque in its honesty and humour. This is juxtaposed by the challenging and difficult story of sexual abuse, which is exposed during the film. Ria, Aditi's cousin refuses to allow her uncle, CI Chadha, who abused her, to abuse the youngest family member Alia. These stories complement the main narrative beautifully with their broken Hinglish, a mixture of Hindi and English in the script.

The film was a success internationally and domestically. Ziya Us Salam in her article 'Desi Spirit in Western Hues' in *The Hindu* newspaper describes how *Monsoon Wedding* acted as the catalyst for launching NRIs into the parallel cinema of India:

> It all started in November last year when cinema-goers invited themselves to Mira Mair's *Monsoon Wedding*. Some just loved it, many enjoyed it, others did not find the attempted bridge between mainstream Hindi cinema and parallel cinema unworthy of a try. (Us Salam, 2002, p. 5)

Salam is right to question the cross-phase success of the film, for it is not a Bollywood film. It has a magical dance scene, but it is sincere and in the context of the narrative, rather than slotted in formulaically to suit the audience's anticipation for five songs and three dances. If audiences wanted a clichéd, yet heart-warming cross-over between Bollywood and Western styles, Gurinder Chadha's 2004 *Bride and Prejudice* would be a far better choice. *Monsoon Wedding* is a well-crafted piece of film. Nair uses hand-held camera work to create the fly on the wall *cinema vérité* sense of being there that really appeals to the atmosphere of the film. Paul Greengrass, a real advocate of this auteur style, never lets the camera rest in the 2004 *The Bourne Supremacy*. His fluid camera work suited the action movie genre perfectly. Nair had to work especially hard to ensure the quality of the film was not compromised by the camera style so she shot on 16mm cine film, which also captured the wonderfully spice-like colour pallet of the sets and the costumes. One key point to also remember is that Nair began her film career as a documentary maker. It might not be surprising, then, that she actually intended to shoot on DV tape, but the vivid colours of her pallet were lost in its inferior quality.

The final word on the film can be given to an unlikely champion of Bollywood cinema, *The Daily Telegraph*. The film's success lay in it its ability to win audiences' hearts and minds because of "its crowd-pleasing ability to sweep an audience into the Punjabi culture of arranged marriages, steady unconsummated teenage lust and the Bacchanalian spirit," it noted (articles.timesofindia.com, 10 September 2001).

What Bollywood did next

Singapore as the backdrop in Krrish

A problem that I found in writing *Studying Bollywood*, was that the Bollywood machine simply works at a frantic pace and even as the book was between drafts it was obvious that an Epilogue was going to be necessary to move the discussion on to where the industry is at the end of the first decade of the twenty-first century . In this final section, then, I will be focusing on two distinct issues that are currently effecting Bollywood. The first is the issue of catering for NRI's and the second is the way the *masala* mix is courting Hollywood and Hollywood stars to inject a new genre into the mix.

At the moment the usual stars that we have already discussed are still in the ascendancy with Amitabh as their stately grandfather. But I will briefly discuss two other actors and how they are striving to draw in NRI audiences. They are India's answer to Jackie Chan, Akshay Kumar, and India's version of the Keanu Reeves character from *The Matrix* (1999), Hrithik Roshan. I don't intend to expand much further as the content and the concept of what Bollywood is as an international film form should be clear at this point. However, a brief look at a couple of their films will be helpful. In fact I finish teaching Bollywood using one of Roshans films, *Krrish* (2006), and so it would be fitting to discuss it here.

Krrish

Rakesh Roshan, who is Hrithik's father, is an established Bollywood director who has acted in, written, composed music for, produced and directed films since the 1970's. His first acting credit was in 1970 and interestingly his last acting credit was in his 2003 film *Koi ...Mil Gaya* (*I Found Someone*) (Roshan, 2003). *Koi... Mil Gaya* was produced and directed by Roshan and starred his son Hrithik the son of a scientist and his wife who are NRIs in Canada.. The child was born a simpleton which was as a result of a car crash during an alien visitation, with many shots reminiscent of the Francis Ford Coppola film *Jack* (1996). Rohit Mehra (Hrithik) is committed to continuing his father's work in communicating with aliens. During this time the film really just turns into a Bollywood version of *E.T.* (1982). The alien in this film is called Jadoo. The film is pretty unmemorable and the effects are also forgettable, they look cheap and far older than of their time. *Krrish* on the other hand is a glossy and exciting text. Sometimes referred to as *Koi... Mil Gaya 2*, this film is a romp and a rip off. It is a romantic romp of a love story, with very strong shades of Clarke Kent and Lois Lane, but in so many ways a rip off of *The Matrix*.

The narrative is not massively important in relation to *Krrish*, in fact I feel the quality of the print and the effects are the aspects the students really are attracted to. *Krrish*, is a Bollywood film but it doesn't look like one, it looks like Hollywood sci-fi. The only problem is that Roshan tries to cram in too many shots of Krrish flying or performing other stunts to the detriment of the narrative. Another very interesting point that the students love is the fact that the majority of the film is based around NRIs based in Singapore. This particular use of the NRIs is designed to sell the film to NRIs across the world. This is helped by the fact that the part of India we do see is geographically anonymous. It is the visiting group of young NRIs form Singapore that are important in the *mise-en-scène*, not India. This, I feel, is a sure sign that Roshan is aiming for the foreign audience's attention.

Krrish prompted some arguments in my classroom; There was a real belief by my students that Roahsn had remixed the *masala* mix, feeling it was a song short. I am not sure that I fully agree, but there is definitely a new dimension to the mix in this film. Rakesh has said previously that the magic to a Bollywood film is how "you position the hero, you have to establish the character, what is he? Where does he stay? Who are his mother and father?"(Ganti, 2004, p. 175). As this is the main focus of *Krrish* the narrative falls in around him. The opening scene of him out-running his horse is a splendid example of Roshan's directorial premise, as is the use of Hrithik's actual double thumb on his right hand, a genuine physical oddity that becomes narratively very important. It is a testament to Hrithik's father that his career has progressed, in an industry where his hand could have realistically nullified his career at the very beginning. Mihir Bose is quite right when he says of Hrithik that "he has a father who can always make movies for him, indicating that Bollywood to a great extent still remains a family business" (Bose, 2006, p. 344).

Akshay Kumar

Akshay Kumar is a revelation in modern Bollywood. He is a whirlwind in his own right, a leading man and the complete all action hero to boot. Kumar has it all, even A-list Hollywood stars who are friends and co-stars, and with the 2009 hit *Blue* (2009) he pulled off the massive coup of securing Kylie Minogue to act and sing in the film. If SRK is the current King of Bollywood, Akshay is the king of crossover as Filmfair put it so well:

> Akshay Kumar's gone from being the Khiladi actor to ruling the roost in the Hindi film industry. He's rolling out hits as if they're made on an assembly line. A move to production was always on the cards. Recently, Akshay set up his production company Hari Om Entertainment and his first film Khatta Meetha with director Priyadarshan is expected to hit the screens later this year. (Filmfare - Business As Usual 1/5, n.d., para. 9)

Namastey London (2007) is probably the best place to start to discuss Akshay as it was a film that uses London and the life of British NRIs as its core plot influence. A sweet comedy, *Namastey London* also stared the beautiful Katarina Kaif and a host of British Indian actors. I don't intend to discuss the plot lines here but it is worth noting that this film's success in the UK helped to endear Akshay to the NRI audience even more. After this success, Akshay started to look further afield, broadening his horizons to draw in Hollywood A-Listers, starting with Snoop Dogg and then Sylvester Stallone.

Askhay was born in 1967 as Rajiv Bhatia and grew up in New Dehli with a large family. He moved to Bangkok to train as a martial arts expert before returning home to work as a chef in a small restaurant. He moved to Bombay in the late eighties and worked as a martial arts trainer until he changed his name and got his big break in 1991 with the flop *Saugandh* (1991). He loves to perform his own stunts, an action that has given him mythical status with his fans. This extreme attitude has made him appealing and alluring to many western actors too.

Kambakkht Ishq (2009) is a film that more than many has shown Akshay's power to influence and attract Hollywood to Bollywood. The film stars Akshay as a Hollywood stunt man and opens with him performing a stunt for *Superman Returns* (2006) star Brandon Routh. The film also stars Sylvester Stallone, one of Akshay's heroes.

But *Blue* is just as important a film for NRIs. *Blue* follows on the back of the film *Singh is Kinng* (2008), a gangster comedy drama set in Australia, where Akshay plays a simpleton who becomes the head of the Australian gangland underworld. The success of Kylie Minogue fused with AR Rahman's music in *Blue* capitalised on *Singh is Kinng* and AR Rahman's growing international fame: "By working with Kylie, I was able to create something truly unique for fans. The music fuses the cultures of mainstream pop, Hindi and Bhangra" (Singh, 2009, para. 1). Kylie said of her role that her "over-riding memory of India is the warmth and professionalism of the people I dealt with whilst making *Blue*. I arrived here as a stranger but I left considering myself as family" (Singh, 2009, para. 2).

Kumar is a huge star and someone who students will identify with as his films (regardless of quality) blend the action of Hollywood with the *masala* mix of Bollywood in a positive and appropriate way.

> Akshay Kumar is perhaps the most reliable or 'saleable' actor in Hindi filmdom today along with Shah Rukh Khan with practically all his films over the last few years taking a huge initial at the box office. What's more he has developed from an action hero in B movies to a reasonably fine actor... And like Shah Rukh, he has made it to the top rung of Bollywood without any 'film' connections whatsoever. (Akshay Kumar | Upperstall.Com, n.d., para. 1)

Bibliography

Akshay Kumar | Upperstall.Com. (n.d.). Upperstall.com. Retrieved July 25, 2010, from http://www.upperstall.com/people/akshay-kumar

Allen, R. (Ed.). (2000). Literature and Nation: Britain and India, 1800 to 1990. London: Routledge in association with The Open University.

Asthana, A. (2009, July 5). Anushka Asthana meets Akshay Kumar, the Bollywood actor whose fame is about to spread to the west | Film | The Observer. theguardian.co.uk. Retrieved July 25, 2010, from http://www.guardian.co.uk/film/2009/jul/05/akshay-kumar-kambakkht-ishq

Barnouw, E. and Krishnaswamy, S. (1980). Indian film. Oxford: Oxford University Press.

Boehmer, E. (1995). Colonial and Postcolonial Literature: migrant metaphors. Oxford: Oxford University Press.

Bose, M. (2006). Bollywood: a history. Stroud Gloucestershire [England]: Tempus Pub.

Cardullo, B. (Ed.). (2007). Satyajit Ray: interviews (1st ed.). Jackson: University Press of Mississippi.

Chopra, A. (2007). King of Bollywood: Shah Rukh Khan and the seductive world of Indian cinema (1st ed.). New York: Warner Books.

Dasgupta, S. (2006). Amitabh: the making of a superstar. New Delhi: Penguin Books.

England, C. (2002). Balham to Bollywood. London: Sceptre.

Filmfare - Business As Usual 1/5. (n.d.). www.filmfair.com. Retrieved July 25, 2010, from http://www.filmfare.com/details.

php?id=1083

Foster, R. (1998). W.B. Yeats: a life. Oxford: Oxford University Press.

Ganti, T. (2004). Bollywood: a guidebook to popular Hindi cinema. London: Routledge.

Gopalan, L. (2005). Bombay. London: British Film Institute.

Howe, D. (1995, June 30). India's Avenging 'Bandit. The Washington Post, 42. Washington.

Jain, M. (2005). The Kapoors: the first family of Indian cinema. New Delhi; New York: Penguin Viking.

Jha, S. (2005). The Essential Guide to Bollywood. New Delhi: Roli Books.

Kabir, N. (2001). Bollywood: the Indian Cinema Story. London: Channel 4 Books.

Kamdar, M. (2007). Planet India: the turbulent rise of the world's largest democracy. London: Simon & Schuster.

Mani Ratnam | Upperstall.Com. (n.d.). Upperstall.com. Retrieved July 22, 2010, from http://www.upperstall.com/people/mani-ratnam

Mohammed, K. (1996, February 14). The Times of India.

Monaco, J. (1981). How to Read a Film: the art, technology, language, history, and theory of film and media (Rev. ed.). New York: Oxford University Press.

Raja, R. (1989). Kanthapura (2nd ed.). Oxford: Oxford University Press.

Sanjeev Kumar | Upperstall.Com. (n.d.). Upperstall.com. Retrieved July 22, 2010, from http://www.upperstall.com/people/sanjeev-kumar

Shekharkapur.com. (n.d.). . Retrieved from http://
shekharkapur.com/blog/

Singh, A. (2009, October 15). Kylie Minogue makes Bollywood
debut with Chiggy Wiggy - Telegraph. telegraph.co.uk.
Retrieved July 25, 2010, from http://www.telegraph.co.uk/
news/newstopics/bollywood/6338490/Kylie-Minogue-makes-
Bollywood-debut-with-Chiggy-Wiggy.html

Stars & Glamour TAG Heuer Ambassadors Shah Rukh Khan
Biography. (n.d.). . Retrieved from http://www.tagheuer.com/
the-brand/stars-tag-heuer/shah-rukh-khan/biography/index.
lbl?lang=en

Swarup, V. (2009). *Q&A* (retitled *Slumdog Millionaire*). London:
Black Swan.

Syal, M., & Bhaskar, S. (1999, November 21). Hooray for
Bollywood! | Film | The Observer. theguardian.co.uk. Retrieved
July 25, 2010, from http://www.guardian.co.uk/film/1999/
nov/21/3

Thompson, K. (2003). Film History: an introduction (2nd ed.).
Boston: McGraw-Hill.

Times of India, 'Mira Nair hailed by UK media', Retrieved July
25, 2010 from http://articles.timesofindia.indiatimes.com/2001-
09-10/news-interviews/27232376_1_monsoon-wedding-
golden-lion-mira-nair

Us Salam, Z. (2002, November 15). The Hindu : Desi spirit in
Western hues. The Hindu. Retrieved from http://www.hindu.
com/thehindu/fr/2002/11/15/stories/2002111500180100.htm